MW01275210

Growing Up
IN
GRANDVIEW

**A three generation story set in
one of Vancouver's pioneer districts
from the turn of the century to the 1950's**

Joan Cupit Proctor

Copyright © 2005 Joan Proctor

All rights reserved. No part of this publication may be reproduced, stored in a retrieval system, or transmitted in any form by any means, electronic, mechanical, photocopy, recording, or otherwise without the prior written permission of the author.

National Library of Canada Cataloguing
In Publication Data

Proctor, Joan, 1938-
Growing Up In Grandview

ISBN 0-9699818-1-3

Production and Design
Gen-X Enterprises
Vancouver, BC Canada

Printed in Canada

Gather the fragments that are left, that nothing may be lost.

-Motto of the Old Cornwall Society

Dedicated with loving memories of my parents
Marion and Arthur Cupit
and grandparents
Grace and Harry Cupit
and
Alice and William Phillifant

I remember, I remember
How my childhood fleeted by,-
The mirth of its December
And the warmth of its July

-Winthrop Mackworth Praed

Contents

Preface

Upon arrival in Vancouver from England in the early 1900's, both sets of my grandparents took up residence in a new district. Having lost much of it's cedar thick woods to the hungry jaws of the Hastings Mill at the foot of Victoria Drive when it had been logged off in the 1890's, the area had gained something, a view!

Once the red interurban train began it's hourly runs, swaying along the tracks from Carrol and Hastings Streets, along Park Drive *(later named Commercial)*, out to New Westminster, the stump laden land gained in appeal. At the top of 1st Avenue and Park where an awesome view of the city had been unlocked, an enthusiastic booster nailed up a sign emblazoned with the words Grand View, and a new suburb was born. Thank goodness he didn't call it Stumpville. Since the name didn't first have to gain approval of a committee, where someone may have insisted upon retaining the original Squamish name Khupkhahpay'ay, which few could have pronounced, let alone market, Grandview it became. Enfolded between the boundaries of Burrard Inlet to the north, Broadway *(9th Avenue)* to the south, Nanaimo Street to the east and Clark Drive to the west, Grandview it has remained, at least in name.

Considered the first dwelling to be constructed in Grandview, a tiny house was built towards the back of a narrow property in the 1600 block of Graveley Street. It was approached by a long straight pathway bordered either side by flowers and lawns. Then a professor of geology and theology, local landowner and promoter Edward Odlum built a splendid turreted house complete with tennis courts on a corner of Grant Street and Commercial. Soon afterwards the area became a popular residential choice as numerous fine domiciles sprung up.

My paternal grandfather born in Lancashire, and my grandmother, born in Cornwall, bought a house on the corner of McLean Drive and Graveley Street. It was just a block from Clark Drive which then overlooked the mud flats of False Creek upon whose frozen waters shore birds and residents, including my father, ice skated in the cold of winter. Yes, Vancouver winters were more frigid then. Panning northwards, the snow-covered Lions looking like a double parfait, provided lofty mountain vistas. My grandparents were to live the rest of their lives at that address, raising five children, one of whom married Jimmy McLarnin, welterweight champion of the world.

A house known at the time of purchase as "the old haunted place," on Venables Street just off Templeton Drive, became home to my maternal grandparents, both from Devon, and their three offspring, all born in Vancouver. When they purchased the place, it had stood abandoned for several years, encroaching bushes either side all but engulfing it. Many windows, broken or boarded up, gave the structure an eerie appearance. Extensive repairs by my grandfather soon made it a showplace. Although he died in 1945, Grandma and her widowed brother whom we called Uncle, lived on at that address until the early 1960's.

These two now nearly century-old homes still stand, but a bungalow with hand-leaded glass windows built in the 1400 block of Graveley Street is gone. Built for my parents by my two grandfathers' and my Dad in 1937, Mom and Dad raised four children there before selling it to new owners in 1971 who demolished it to make way for an apartment.

With its beautiful iron tracery balconies, Grandview United, the church we regularly attended, once boasted a congregation of 800 souls. Standing almost at the corner of Venables Street and Victoria Drive, it is now the Vancouver East Cultural Center. Woodland Elementary School that I attended for six years is today a First Nations School called Uuqinak'uuh, and Britannia, my old high school has become a varied community center. The Grandview Highschool of Commerce on 1st Avenue between Cotton and Commercial Drives once housed Arthur Delamont's famed Kitsilano Boys Band for their weekly practices in a structure near the back alley. Torn down in 1954, the site now holds Il Mercato.

Parks such as Grandview and Victoria where verdant stretches of lawn bordered by azaleas and rhododendrons once enclosed tennis courts and lawn bowling, have now mostly been reduced to sandlots for ball. Blocks of once fine homes were turned into more profitable suites or demolished to make room for stuccoed apartments and condominiums. As industry crept in and the sky train clattered above, the old Grandview vanished.

There was a time when Vancouver's self-sufficient districts were reminiscent of villages and Grandview in the early days could have been lifted from England, for most of its inhabitants had hailed from the motherland. Surnames of residents reflected that heritage, as did those of the street-names in the district. Gardens with borders of English flowers abounded behind clipped boxwood hedges and properties treed with monkey-puzzle, hawthorn and oak.

This was an era when most needs were easily met by the numerous shops rimming Commercial Drive. Physicians had offices in their homes, and there were several private hospitals in the neighborhood. Churches represented most of the major religions and schools provided education from elementary through high school. Thus, Grandview's residents rarely needed to bother with a trip down town. It was possible to be born, live and die in the enclave.

My growing up years in Grandview took place in the 1940's and 50's before it became known as Little Italy, but when the face of our neighborhood was swiftly altering, changing the appearance of our "English" village forever.

- Joan Cupit Proctor

Part 1

Growing Up In Grandview

Chapter 1

Yesterday's Birds

When I was a little girl sitting demurely at my Grandma Alice Phillifant's dining room table sipping what she called Cambric Tea from a pretty bone china cup, a thought came to me. "Grandma," I asked, "Who was your Grandma"?

"She was a Bird," came the reply. "Now drink your tea my dear."

A bird? The idea seemed pretty funny and I covered my snickerings with a small cupped left hand, then braved another question. "Where did she live?"

"Back home in Plymouth," answered Grandma, adding "she was a tiny little lady, gone to her reward now." She sighed before continuing, "Yes, all the Birds have gone to heaven."

At Grandview United Church Sunday School that week we sang God Sees the Little Sparrow Fall, it meets His tender view. When we came to the line, if God so loves the little birds I know He loves me too, I thought of tiny Great Great Grandma Bird and sang out extra loud! Maybe, I thought, she could hear me from heaven. And maybe she did.

Eighty-four years before my birth in Vancouver, a tiny blonde haired, blue eyed girl was born to Edwin and Emma Bird in Plymouth, England. It was April, 1854, and they named her Emma Jane. A mere month had passed since Britain and France had declared war on Russia. The Crimean War, with one of its heroes being the British nurse Florence Nightingale *(who had nothing to do with our Birds)* would be a major turning point in the political history of post Napoleonic Europe. Although sadly, I cannot put names to them, some male members of the Bird family were part of the British forces who lost their lives fighting at the Battle of Inkerman, which ended November, 1854, the last of the 3 battles preceding the long siege of Sebastopol.

Thirty-five-year old Queen Victoria was on the throne and in the United States they had elected their 14th president, Franklin Pierce. In Canada, still consisting of Upper and Lower Colonies, the Reciprocity Treaty was signed with the United States. This saw the beginning of immigration of cheap labor, the building of railways and commercial and industrial development. It was also a year in which a mining engineer named Grant reported to the London Geographical Society on the discovery of coal deposits found along the shore of Burrard Inlet which in 1792 had been named by Captain George Vancouver for his friend Sir Harry Burrard. Herds of elk still roamed the future Grandview known at this time as Khupkhahpayay, the Squamish word for cedar, for the area abounded in it. The fragrant conifers supplied the natives with materials for everything from homes and canoes to woven baskets. And at the northern foot of what would become Victoria Drive, a small creek emptying quietly into a Burrard Inlet bay would soon be known as Cedar Cove.

Not much is known of the early days of the Bird family consisting of daughter Emma and siblings John, Amy, Thomas and Bessie aside from the fact the children received schooling and religious education. Therefore we'll fast forward to the year 1872 when auburn haired Emma, now 18, married John Josiah Warne, a 19 year old lad of fair complexion and pale blue eyes, from a seafaring family. Although I'm certain no one informed them, the April 24th date of the young couple's wedding marked the flying of the first Canadian flag in far off Burrard Inlet over a hotel known as Deighton House. It was in Gastown, and British Columbia had entered Confederation just nine months earlier. The first school had also opened that year on Hastings Mill property and construction had begun on the Yale Wagon Road which would one day link the Lower Mainland to the B.C. Interior.

We now return to Plymouth, birthplace of Sir Francis Drake whose fleet sailed to meet the Spanish Armada in 1588 and renowned for the embarkation of the Pilgrims who sailed to America on the Mayflower in 1620. But that's another story. Suffice to say the famed port had spawned many a navy man and the Warnes' were no exception. John's father, a British sailor had been lost at sea and his remains never found. This meant his wealth was held in the Chancellery for many years making life financially difficult for his widow and family. A further complication lay in the fact John was partially deaf from a childhood disease, and so instead of joining the Royal Navy for a roustabout life on the bounding main, he was apprenticed to a cooper where he learned to make casks and barrels.

In an era when most goods were shipped this way, *(tight, used for spirits and acids)* or slack which were filled with dry goods, this was considered a lucrative trade. A cooper's wages *(after the apprenticeship)* brought him about $2.00 per day.

Emma and John's first child, John Henry who would be known as Jack, was born February, 1875 and seventeen months later a daughter Emma Jane was born. The birth of another son Alfred Edwin, in May, 1881 happened to coincide with a story appearing in a London newspaper stating, "British Columbia is a barren, cold, mountain country that is not worth keeping." Perhaps the reporter had glimpsed what would soon become known as Grandview, a once heavily forested area that had only recently been stripped of vast stands of enormous cedars, firs and hemlocks, logged off by the Hastings Sawmill Company. Only stumps of considerable girth now bore quiet testimony to what had been. And by this time the last of the great herds of elk had vanished... thirteen of them cut down by Chief Joe Capilano who canoed the meat to a Victoria market where he stood to make a nice little profit.

When Alice, the youngest of the Warne children, opened her blue eyes to the world on St. George's Day, 1885 in Devonport, England, it was the year the automobile industry dawned upon the world with the development by Daimler and Benz of the first complete three wheeled automobile. And as if wheels weren't enough, on November 7, 1885, far across the snow dusted Rocky Mountains of British Columbia, The Last Spike of the Canadian Pacific Railway was driven at Craigelachie by Lord Strathcona who would have a neighborhood and school named for him in Vancouver's east end. Little did the Warne family of Plymouth know, their little Alice would be destined to one day travel that railway across Canada to make her home with a young Devonshireman from Lifton Downs.

But life's no pudding full of plums, and on Christmas Eve 1885 disaster struck the diminutive five foot tall Emma, when her husband John was carried home suffering from a head injury. He and some fellow workers having perhaps partaken of some Christmas cheer decided to take a short cut home that evening to make up for lost time. As they crossed the frost-covered marble steps of Plymouth's Post Office, John slipped and fell, striking his head. He lingered for days, lying on a bed in their front parlor a true victim of the dead letter office, never regaining consciousness before dying. He was 30 years old. Emma was left with the four children ranging in age from eight month old Alice to ten-year old Jack, a promising student who now had to leave school and become an errand boy to help provide for his mother and three siblings.

Young Jack, would later apprentice as a mason in 1886, the same year that halfway around the world on June 13th the newly incorporated city of Vancouver burned to the ground. Rebounding however with amazing vigor, this was the same city where by 1887 Engine #374 *(The Puffing Billy)* Canada's most famous steam engine pulled the first passenger train into town on C PR's newly completed transcontinental railway.

In 1889, as Jack's apprenticeship continued, a famous author, Rudyard Kipling visited and became a landholder in Vancouver. He was quoted as saying, "Such a land is good for an energetic man. It is also not so bad for a loafer." In Plymouth however, no loafing was going on in the Warne household. Jack's sister Em and brother Alfred stayed in school, but their mother went to work as a machinist in a garment factory and young Alice was looked after by whichever relative was available until the family moved to their Uncle William's house. A barrister, he was very proud of the engraved brass name plate on his front door stating his position. It had to be polished daily and later became one of Alice's hated jobs. He lived extravagantly and enjoyed the good things in life before losing much of his fortune, perhaps to riotous living. Whatever the reason, whether for financial gain or, giving him the benefit of doubt, out of the goodness of his heart, Uncle William turned his home into three suites. Two aunties, Amy and Bessie who worked from home as dressmakers and machinists took the top floor, Emma and her four children the middle floor, and William the main floor. Living beneath a family of four children could not have been easy on him, even before the days of television sets and loud stereos when children were supposed to be seen but not heard. The sound of hob-nailed boots on his ceiling may not have been conducive to studying his law books.

Alice, with her blue eyes and dark curly hair, was adored by all... watched over by the two doting aunties during the days and given much attention from her two brothers and sister. By the time she was required to go to school however, this spoiled little girl found things not so easy. Fun-loving, but strong-willed she soon tired of the strictness that prevailed and began a profitable but short-lived venture of her own. This was a period when schooling had to be paid for on a daily basis. She would be given tuppence for the day's tuition, but often played hooky and spent the cash. Then when found out, she'd be escorted home by the truant officer. They didn't mess around in those days! The auntie's finally wised up, and paid the money themselves a week in advance. This didn't foil Alice from developing a cunning plan. Enroute to school she would pick flowers, mint and parsley from various gardens along the way, bundle them and then sell them to her partner in crime, the local butcher's shop, for money which she then used to buy sweets. The bewildered ladies couldn't keep up with her.

Amy and Bessie were spinsters and neither had the slightest idea of how to deal with a high-spirited girl. But Alice had a reflective side too. When one of her uncle's presented her with a canary which prematurely went to meet it's maker, she tenderly lined a tiny box with mauve satin, placed the deceased bird inside and buried it in the garden complete with a bird adorned hat pin for a marker and hand-lettered epitaph which read, "Sing sweetly birdie, for now you're in heaven".

The family dwelling in Plymouth was built over the subterranean tunnels once used by smugglers and pirates. Hollowed into the cliffs along the Atlantic coastline of England, these hiding places once held booty confiscated from sailing ships. One story often repeated was that a series of these interconnecting tunnels actually led from beneath the Warne family's home all the way out to the foot of Drake's Column, a well-known and revered piece of Plymouth history. In the years that Alice was growing up, the family used the pockets beneath the house as a kind of root cellar or cooler where their perishables were stored. On one occasion when Alice was sent below to fetch a jug of cream, she decided it was so dark and spidery down there, she would light a candle, flashlights having not yet been invented. There were gasses in the caverns and "she very nearly blew us all to Kingdom Come!" I recall Uncle *(Jack)* saying many years later.

Because many of the male members of the family, *(cousins and uncles)*, were in the Navy at a time when Britain truly ruled the waves, numerous interesting treasures brought home from exotic ports found their way into the Warne's abode along with a noisy parrot that lived out a long life in their front parlor. This crusty parrot had an interesting vocabulary which combined sprinklings of seafarer's cursings with a few lines of Glory, Glory Hallelujah which he purportedly "sang" although raspily, right on key.

One fine day "our little pet" as Alice was sometimes referred to, decided to dress up in Aunt Amy's best cape and bonnet. Black kid-gloves were taken from her bandbox to accessorise the outfit along with a ruffle-edged black parasol. Off she trotted, to the grand promenade known as The Hoe, which seemed to be one of her favorite haunts. Upon her return, there at the door, hands planted firmly on hips, was a stern faced Aunt Amy who had watched the entire scenario and was anything but pleased as she retrieved her street soiled attire.

Alice turned 14 in the spring of 1899, as the world's tallest structure, The Eiffel Tower, was featured at the Universal Exhibition in Paris and written about in newspapers worldwide. At the other extreme, far away in Vancouver, a tiny wooden house in the 1600 block on a street called Graveley became the first dwelling in a new district in sight of a picturesque mountain range. It was named Grandview! Now with an interurban railway running from Vancouver to New Westminster along Park Drive (later Commercial Drive) many people saw the areas potential.

By autumn of that same year as the leaves bronzed and murky fogs gathered over Plymouth Harbour a more serious mood prevailed when the Boer War broke out and troops of British men were sent to "uphold Britain's honor" in the Transvaal, *(South African Republic)*. One young man who answered the call was Fred Phillifant, from a large family in Devon. He and Em the eldest daughter of the Warne children were keeping company and were engaged to marry just before he left for Africa.

Jack, now 24, was working as a mason, and had become a member of the Guild. I remember the large framed certificate attesting to this, his name illuminated in gold. It hung on one of his bedroom walls, a proud possession brought from Plymouth to Vancouver where in November of 1900 this excerpt from The Province newspaper appeared:

> *"On the sunny slope which dips with gentle undulations into the golden west, and commands an exquisite panoramic eyeshot of the Gulf of Georgia, the mountains of Vancouver Island and Howe Sound, softly blue in the enchanted distance, the well-to-do of Vancouver have pitched their tents, and settled down amid surroundings the most salubrious and beautiful. Here they have transformed what was ten years ago, a virgin forest, where the salmon berry, the salal, the huckleberry and the succulent skunk cabbage flourished. Where once and not so long ago, the dusky Abigails of the Siwash camps threaded their way through tangled woodland paths in pursuit of the coy and retiring blackberry, of which to sell to the strange pie-eating paleface now flaunts milady in silk attire, her circumambient atmosphere of frangipani or jockey club gratefully replacing the klootchman's abiding aroma of long-landed fish.*
>
> *"No more the evening fires of the red man ascend on rainless summer evenings from that patrician quarter, in thin blue spirals, into the glowing sunset; for the mansions of the tyhees amongst the newcomers in this land of golden opportunities now occupy the happy hunting grounds of the nomadic children of forest and stream. Now is the glorious clam-guzzle of the years gone by, superseded by the progressive euchre party, the stag dinner, the ice cream and souffle after the ball. The transformation has been complete. Vancouver attracts the admiring attention of the cultured stranger, and high praise is heard when its residential architecture is mentioned."*

A New Year's Eve Grand Fancy Ball was taking place December 31st, 1900 at London's Covent Garden offering 6 special and 16 other valuable prizes to those in attendance. And in the Daily Mail there were ads for a Children's Pantomime, "The Sleeping Beauty and The Beast" at the Drury Lane Theatre while at The Savoy, every evening at 8:30 Gilbert and Sullivan's "Patience" was being staged to gales of laughter from audiences as duets like "High diddle diddle will rank as an idyll, if I pronounce it chaste!" rang out.

In London and South West England where the Warne's lived, strong northerly winds brought cold showers which quickly turned to sleet, then snow on New Years Day, Tuesday January 1st. Meanwhile, in faraway Vancouver, the residents had greeted the new century waking to over a foot of snow. Except for the sound of sleigh bells on some streets, all lay still, clothed in spotless white, the forests of firs and cedars bent beneath their snowy mantles. By January 22nd with the death after a 69 year reign, of Queen Victoria, the Edwardian era was ushered in when her son Edward VII and his wife Alexandra ascended the throne.

School was not working out, or more to the point, Alice was not working in school, so was allowed to begin apprenticing as a milliner. The Edwardian epoch was a time when a proper hat for a proper lady was a work of art. Recall the hats worn by the ladies in the Ascot scene of the movie, My Fair Lady, and you'll get the picture. The more elaborate the better. Alice was wonderful at creating hats. She was also wonderful at "borrowing" hats from the shop where she worked or from her sister Em's wardrobe and wearing them on, yes indeed... Plymouth Hoe, where she paraded with her friends after chapel. Whether it was on the famed Hoe, *(where Drake played bowls as the Spanish Armada hove in sight)* or elsewhere, she caught the eye of a young sailor with whom she became enamoured, and he likewise.

Meanwhile sister Em, had sailed off to South Africa to marry Fred Phillifant. When the ship reached Africa it had to anchor some distance from shore. Passengers were then conveyed from ship to shore in a large basket on cables. When it was Em's turn she was frightened and refused to get into the wicker container despite the fact her intended was waiting on shore. After much cajoling from the ship's officer's she remained adamant; she was not getting into that basket. There was no alternative but to toss her bodily into the contraption and send her flailing and screaming on her way. *Hail the bridegroom, hail the bride!* She made it, only to discover once ashore, that Fred had neglected to buy a wedding band. She refused to stay with him until they were properly churched. A hastily arranged ceremony took place using a borrowed ring from the minister's wife. They eventually immigrated to the exciting new city of Vancouver on Canada's Pacific Coast where the only baskets in sight were those carried on poles by Chinese fishermen.

So it was that when Tom gave Alice a ring set with three sparkling diamonds and a promise of marriage when he returned from sea she had dreams of wedded bliss as the wife of a British tar. He sailed to the Orient on the same ship as her brother Alfred, also now in the Royal Navy. On a postcard sent to her from Gibraltar he thanks her for some books saying they will suit him very much and that he always did say that she had very good taste and that the books she selected are just his style. Signed, "I am yours, Tom".

In June of 1905 Jack Warne married Helen Jane Blight, in the parish church of Morval, Cornwall, just north of the south coast fishing port of Looe, an area of rolling countryside where canal boats would come up the river to Sandplace *(Helen's birthplace)* to drop off cargoes of seaweed which would be spread on the verdant fields before returning with cargoes of lime from the kilns.

Helen, a tall slim girl with light brown hair and wide set - blue eyes had attended the Morval Parochial School where among other proper lessons of the period, she learned the art of stitchery, practising on samplers signed with her maiden name in fine embroidery thread.

Although his home base was with his mother Emma in Plymouth, Jack often worked away in other towns or cities such as

Liverpool or Manchester. Through the years the couple kept up a correspondence by postcards which she secured in a green leather bound album, a quiet testimony to their love for one another.

Jack sang in church choirs as well as many of the days popular Gilbert and Sullivan Operettas. He had a lovely clear tenor voice, and I need only close my eyes and think back to hear him singing by the piano in my Grandma's living room," She was the perfect daughter of a perfect major general" *(from HMS Pinafore)* or the lovely hymn Still, still with Thee when purple morning breaketh. Brightest and Best *(a hymn for Epiphany)* was another of his favorites.

Following their marriage, with constant exciting news from family members and friends residing in Vancouver about the abundance of work and promise of wealth to be made there, Jack and Helen made the decision to emmigrate at the first opportunity. Doctors had imprudently suggested the Pacific climate might be better for Helen's frail health. Obviously they didn't know about the preponderance of rain, fog and general dampness and were thinking perhaps of that other pacific clime known as the South Pacific. Someone should have produced a map.

Jack would go to Vancouver and establish himself, buying a house on Eton Street next door to his sister Em and her husband Fred, then send for Helen who in the meantime would stay in their Plymouth residence. By February she would ship 3 cases of their goods on the S S Bellerophon from Liverpool to Canada. Amongst these possessions, a blue china clock from Paris and pair of cobalt urns.

About this time Tom, Alice's sea faring fiancée sent word he'd missed the sailing when his ship was due to return to England from the Orient. It was considered he had jumped ship and he was therefore disgraced. He now had no way to get home. In vain, he tried for several months to persuade Alice into sailing to the Orient to marry him. She would have nothing of it. He'd missed the boat in more ways than one! Having broken their engagement Alice was faced with moping about or, visiting her sister and brother-in-law in Canada. In an effort to mend her broken heart, she chose the latter. Her brother Alf now in Jerusalem sent her a farewell gift, a Bible and book entitled Flowers of the Holy Land both beautifully encased between olive wood covers with intricate inlaid patterns. Truly works of art they were long treasured by her.

Chapter 2

From Atlantic To Pacific

Travelling by train from Plymouth to Liverpool on April 7th Alice boarded the recently launched Virginian, a 540-foot ship belonging to the famed Allan Line. Making headlines in the newspapers, along with her sister ship the Victorian, these ships and The Empresses of Britain, and Ireland from Canadian Pacific's All Red Route fulfilled the mail contract from Liverpool to Quebec with weekly service round trips. The first turbine liner on the Atlantic, the Virginian carried 1650 passengers on five decks, all of which were heated and ventilated on the thermos tank system with individual cabin control, something new for the day. In advertisements of the period, even 3rd class accommodations were touted: *- Hot water is provided, and is always on tap, so that "Lady Thirds" who wish to dispense the kindly cup of afternoon tea to their fellow voyagers have always the means of doing so.*

Whether Alice was one of the lady thirds, or was able to travel with a little more style, I've no idea, but it must have been quite an adventure for an unaccompanied young lady sailing first out into the Irish Sea and then steaming at a sustained sea speed of 17 knots across the Atlantic and eventually up the St. Lawrence River to Montreal.

It was a warm spring day in 1905 when Alice arrived in Vancouver to be met by Em, Fred and their three year old daughter Elsie at the Caledonian Chateau styled CPR building which then stood at the north foot of Granville Street. Besides the long trip over the Atlantic she'd also endured a week's train travel from Montreal to the Pacific Coast. There she found a seaport city with a harbor destined to take it's place in the world just as her hometown of Plymouth with it's renowned natural harbor had done. Lot values were among the highest on the continent and there were no fewer than 50 real estate agents in the town. The city population at 45,000 was less than half that of Plymouth. Being the last stop on the Transcontinental railway, Vancouver was the place to go if you wanted to get rich. Borrowing a phrase from Alan Morley's book *Vancouver from Milltown to Metropolis,* 'LAND, LAND, LAND! BUY A LOT TODAY-BE A MILLIONAIRE TO-MORROW!' Morley says, "These were the new city's golden years. Towers, turrets, battlements, gingerbread work, monkey puzzle trees, clipped hollies and Chinese house boys were the norm in the wealthy west-end while gentlemen in bowler hats crowded the streets of the business districts and ladies decked out in proper riding gear drove tandem rigs around Stanley Park."

Although paved sidewalks were appearing, in most areas they were still constructed of wooden planks and roads of dirt were the norm. Crossing the street on a rainy day could prove deadly. If the mud and potholes didn't get you, you were also in danger of being run down by one of the main methods of transportation. Horses and buggies or bicycles were the accepted way of getting around unless you used the streetcars which ran on the main thoroughfares only. Generally, the way to get anywhere was "shanks mare" an old saying that meant on foot. Some of the city's landmark's still surviving were there when Alice first saw Vancouver. The Hudsons Bay Store stood on the corner of Georgia and Granville where once 310 foot tall trees had towered, the Carnegie Library straddled the corner of Main and Hastings, the Holland Block graced Water Street, and the big red "W" acted like a homing beacon atop Woodward's store on Hastings and Abbott. Boasting 18 fireplaces in it's wood-paneled interiors, the Rogers mansion at 1523 Davie Street had just been built by sugar tycoon B. T. Rogers. In Stanley Park the nine o'clock gun, a cast-iron muzzle-loader from Woolwich, England was already a landmark at Hallelujah Point, a little piece of land near Brockton Point so named because that was where the Salvation Army held summer picnics. The lighthouse and foghorn had already been established there since 1890. And at English Bay if you didn't want to stroll along the new pier you could sit on one of the huge rocks that dotted the beach at low-tide and watch Edwardian celebrity, Barbados born Joe Fortes, self-proclaimed and unpaid lifeguard, showing children how to swim.

Chapter 3

Thatching To Match-Making

Fred Phillifant's younger brother William was also living in Vancouver taking advantage of the building whirl along with two colleagues. And so it was that the Phillifant brothers, Fred and William and the Kallaway brothers Harold and Jimmy began their own construction business building houses in Cedar Cove overlooking Burrard Inlet from Wall Street up to East Hastings between Nanaimo and Renfrew where the streets are named after universities: Yale, Trinity, McGill, Eton, Cambridge and Oxford. One of young William's specialties was architectural detailing, popular at this time when the Queen Anne style house with its ornate bargeboards, brackets, corbels and gables was fashionable in Vancouver neighborhoods.

It wasn't too long before Alice, residing at Em and Fred's home on Eton Street, became enamoured of William, and he with her in a romance duly encouraged by her sister and his brother who evidently thought it an ideal match. Besides, it would take the stress of worrying about Alice off Em's shoulders and settle young Will down. Not that he was anxious to tie the knot at this point. There were a number of young ladies who had their eye on him. He was a lot of fun to be with. Marriage, it seems was not something he was overly anxious to embark upon.

William or Will as he was always called, was the youngest son of a family of 11 children and had come to Vancouver in 1900 at the age of 19 from the tranquil little village of Lifton Downs in Devon, England where his father John, whom he called Da was a roof thatcher. Considered the best for miles around, people would often wait weeks just to have John Phillifant do their roof. Ellen Mitchell Phillifant, John's wife had been born in Guinear, Cornwall. As Will's sister, Matilda said, "it broke our mother's heart when her Will sailed for Canada." She gave him a tiny book just 2 ½ by 3 inches entitled Home and Heaven. A black and white photo of a stone bridge in Lifton adorned the cover and inside was a poem by James Montgomery and 31 pages; one for each day of the month with a short scripture reading and a thought for the day such as the following: - *"Oh, far from home thy footsteps stray, Christ is the life and Christ the way."* There was great love between them, but like so many other young lads, Will left England for Canada because of the opportunities awaiting him in Vancouver where he stood to make a good living doing something he liked. If he'd stayed in Devon he'd have had to help his father in the roof thatching trade, or perhaps follow in his grandfather's footsteps spending his life as a gardener on one of Lifton's large estates. A new start in a young Pacific coast city definitely had appeal.

Will may have been a passenger on either The Tunisian or Parisian as both were ships sailing between Liverpool and Montreal at that period. They had 4 berth emigrant cabins complete with spring mattresses and passengers could reach any part of the extensive public rooms without going on deck. Considered good looking ships that "truly belonged to the 20th century, they marked a departure from sailing-ship thinking". From Montreal, the young men made their way across the vast country to the still mostly untamed west coast destination of Vancouver.

Although only 5'5" in height, Will was *(to use Alice's own words)* "a charmer" with his dark, flashing eyes, thick dark hair and moustache. Along with designing, inventing and creating things, he loved carpentry work, the outdoors and the new land. He and the Kallaway brothers bached in a small house of their own at Cedar Cove, but there were many family get-togethers with Emma, Fred, Alice, Jack and Helen. Will had a small boat which held six and they would all pile into it and row across Burrard Inlet to the green forests of the North Shore, travelling up Lynn Creek where they would go hiking and picnicking in Lynn Canyon and Will would take photographs, another of his interests. Usually his subjects were pictured wearing their Sunday best in sylvan settings, often perched incongruously as well as precariously on huge felled trees or the edge of a roaring waterfall. How the ladies managed to traverse streams and heavily wooded areas in their long skirts and crisp white blouses I'll never know. They seemed always to keep their hats on too. Will enjoyed soloing on numerous sketching painting trips around Capilano Canyon, another favorite haunt. At one time there seemed to be so many paintings he'd done of the second canyon, Capilano that someone likened his fixation with Monet's Waterlillies. Perhaps he was just trying to get it right.

Stanley Park, with it's 1,000 acres of primeval forest, was another place he frequented, pulling his boat up to the rocky shore between what is now Brockton Point and Lumberman's Arch where he visited and was friends with the Squamish who lived in little houses that then dotted the beach. The area was known as Whoi Whoi. As a child, I remember going always to that exact section of waterfront with our family, where by then only two of the native dwellings remained on the beach. At least once a week right up until the latter part of the 1950's we went to *that spot*. By then the seawall, begun in 1917, was mostly in place and we'd often just sit on it listening to the tune of the waves, which depending on the weather could be gently lapping or pounding with staccato-like force. We called it "our beach" and were quite put out if ever anyone else was there, an unlikely situation in those quiet days before the Park became overpopulated and under-treed, and parking meters made their appearance along that once pristine stretch. I can understand now why that section of beach became so dear to us, for having been one of my Grandpa Will's beloved areas it was almost as if it was bequeathed to us in spirit afterwards.

By 1910 Vancouver's population had quadrupled to 100,000. There was lots of work. Things were going well. A new Opera House was near completion on Granville Street where now a bridge had opened to automobile traffic that still drove on the left side as in Britain. In the new district of Grandview, so named because of it's breath-catching view of the North Shore Mountains, large homes were appearing with wrap around porches, turreted towers, widows walks and fern filled conservatories. Grandview encompassed the area between Burrard Inlet to the north, Broadway (9th Avenue) to the south with Nanaimo Street it's eastern border and Clark Drive it's west. On the corner of Victoria Drive and Venables Street, Grandview Methodist Church opened its doors. And on sun-filled summer days yachts glided over Coal Harbor and dotted English Bay, while people in their whites lawn bowled and cheers cracked the air at the cricket match. Will and Alice had now been keeping company for nearly five years. When he finally proposed marriage, Alice stubbornly decided to return to England "to think about it." Ever the optimist, Will gave her a handcrafted wooden trunk that he'd made complete with her initials A.W. hand cut in brass upon its lid for the return voyage. Always the romantic, Will placed a note inside the trunks lid.

> *Go search the world and search the sea, Then come you home and sing with me. There's no such gold and no such pearl as a bright and beautiful English girl!*
> *- from Act 2 of Gilbert and Sullivan's Utopia*

He then began to build a house for them on Prince Albert Street in the district of Cedar Cottage.

Chapter 4

Plymouth And Pledges

Once back in Plymouth Alice missed Will terribly and knew she was destined to return to Vancouver to marry him. But in those days, and with limited resources, one couldn't just pick up and travel easily, so she stayed a year.

She spent her time getting her trousseau ready and saying her good-byes to family and girlhood friends like Beattie Pomeroy whose wedding in St. Andrew's Church, Plymouth Alice attended, and with whom she would maintain correspondence until both were in their nineties.

While Alice was enjoying her year back in England, Emma, her mother having already faced saying good-bye to Jack, Helen, Em and Fred, realized soon her youngest daughter would also be gone. This would leave only Alfred in England, and being in the navy he was often far away for months on end. As she helped sew her daughter's wedding dress, it must have been difficult knowing most of her children were putting down roots in a faraway Pacific Coast city she would never visit. At the end of June she held Alice close to her heart for the last time, stroking her long black hair as they kissed good-bye and she watched her sail from her life and the Liverpool berth. What a lonely train journey back to Plymouth she must have had. They would never again see one another.

On a warm July 29th, 1911 in Vancouver, William and Alice were married in Dundas Presbyterian Church although ironically neither were Presbyterians. He was Church of England and she was Methodist. However, since Will had done most of the building on the little church named for the street on which it stood, and the minister had become quite fond of him he suggested they be the first couple married there. Alice wore the garnet colored suit with amethyst tucked satin blouse, (a seemingly inappropriate choice for a hot July day), her mother's gold heart bracelet and her Grandma Bird's pearl brooch. A very large hat, the brim lined with amethyst silk and tiny English violets rested on her upswept hair. Yes, she had fashioned the hat herself. Giving equal attention to Will, he is pictured with handlebar moustache, looking extremely dapper although a little solemn in white tie and tails.

The Reverend E.H. Lockhart who married them, gave them an inscribed bible for a wedding gift and her brother Jack gave her in marriage. Thus with two Warne sisters wed to two Phillifant brothers, the families would be inexorably linked. The little church, scene of their nuptials still stands today in east Vancouver although not on its original site. Years later it was moved to another address up above Nanaimo Street in a feat accomplished by rolling logs beneath the structure bit by bit, inching it slowly along the dirt roads to it's new location. As a kid I remember every time we drove past it we were reminded by our Mother, "there's the church that your Grandpa built." As we were also told this about Vancouver's Marine Building and other landmarks that our paternal grandfather worked on, we figured the two of them pretty well built the city.

When Will and Alice moved into their first home in the district of Cedar Cottage, then at the end of the interurban line, it was a bustling neighborhood with it's own commercial street consisting of a bank, movie theatre, lumber yard and roller coaster! On July

18, 1912 their first child, dark haired, brown eyed Marion Louise was born. Christened in a hand made gown sent from her grandmother, Emma in Plymouth, she also wore a tiny gold cross on a fine chain, a gift from the loving Grandma and two great aunties, Amy and Bessie none of whom she would ever meet.

The year 1912 saw the opening of the newly constructed landmark building at the corner of Beatty and Pender Streets for the newspaper, The Vancouver World, *(later becoming premises for Bekins Moving and Storage when its backers went broke, and then The Sun)*. At a mind-boggling 17 stories high this structure-eclipsed Vancouver's first skyscraper, The Dominion Trust Building, on Hastings and Cambie, which until then at 14 stories had been the tallest building in the British Empire. The B.C. Electric Building at the corner of Carrall and Hastings made it's appearance operating the most extensive interurban tramway system in Canada. The Vancouver Block with it's distinctive four -sided clock tower and white ceramic sheathing drew oohs and ahhs from citizens, but the fire department was still using horse-drawn wagons. A visit by the Duke and Duchess of Connaught in September saw them riding by automobile through the newly erected Lumberman's Arch which then stood at Pender and Hamilton. But in world news, the sinking of The Titanic that year eclipsed all else.

People mainly got around Vancouver at this time by walking or using the extensive streetcar system with the interurban carrying passengers out to New Westminster or Cedar Cottage. Alice's prized Austrian china dinner set *(white with pink rosebuds)* called Victoria, was purchased at Millar and Coe's a popular fine china and house wares shop on Hastings Street not far from Woodward's and brought home by Will in two string shopping bags on the interurban. For the uninitiated, string bags were a type of shopping bag of the era, which although small enough to roll up and place in one's pocket, had the ability to stretch to unbelievably heroic dimensions as items were placed in them. When one considers the set included eight complete place settings plus vegetable dishes and three sizes of platters, getting it home unbroken on a swaying interurban train was admirable.

Districts were springing up like wildfire... Kitsilano, Fairview, and Grandview inside the city limits while Kerrisdale, Cedar Cottage and Collingwood were in South Vancouver. Workers settled in South Vancouver, the middle classes in Kitsilano and Kerrisdale while the wealthy lived in the West End.

False Creek at this time extended as far east as Clark Drive, named for an early developer who donated a block of land for a park also named after him in 1899 making it the city's second park after Stanley Park, and west to Westminster Avenue *(later renamed Main Street)*.

In March 1914 Will and Alice's second daughter, fair-haired Muriel Vivian was born. They were still living in the house out in South Vancouver at this time, but now things were not going well in the construction business, and Will found himself overextended. They lost their house on Prince Albert Street and for a time lived in a rented house on 1st Avenue, just above Victoria Drive, before moving to a smaller home at 2316 Wall Street over looking Burrard Inlet. They were now back in the Cedar Cove area where not only Will had started out upon arrival in Vancouver, but where historical Hastings Townsite, one of the earliest Lower Mainland communities had it's beginnings. This neighborhood had been the scene of the first cricket ground, first pier, first store and first hotel. For this little family however, the years on Wall Street would be a challenge. A depression had hit Vancouver. The housing market was non-existent. Many businesses from the Dominion Trust Company to suburban merchants suffered financial collapse and the city soon filled with unemployed men. It seemed the boom days were coming to a close. On the corner of West Hastings and Hornby however, a new edifice constructed of ten stories of finely cut stone opened as Credit Foncier of Montreal came to Vancouver. And at the other extreme, a whimsical new band stand of cedar complete with cupola now graced Alexandra Park at English Bay, where people would sit upon lawns strewn with English daisies on sunny Sunday afternoons listening to band music, trying hard to forget their troubles.

Chapter 5

The End Of The Halcyon Days

Recruiting tents went up across Canada in August that year after Great Britain had declared war on Germany. Believing the conflict would be over by Christmas, thousands signed up. By October the first Canadian contingent consisting of 33,000 men, 7,000 horses and 144 pieces of artillery had left for England; the largest armed force to cross the ocean at that time. The halcyon days were over.

Will, now had great difficulty finding carpentry work. He did odd jobs for people often accepting things other than cash as payment. The family had their own garden, chickens, geese and rabbits, but it was a real struggle and Will was always bringing some poor soul home for a free meal which further taxed Alice. Her sister Em, always kindhearted, would tell her to just make do by throwing some more water in the stew, but Alice failed to see the humor. On one occasion when he'd finally made some decent money Will spent most of it on a dainty gold bracelet with tiny pearl set flowers and delicate chain clasp. She wept when she received it, saying the money could have been better spent. But he talked her into keeping it, as with a garnet and pearl brooch purchased just before he told her his news. He'd enlisted in the army.

With no work, Will and his brother Fred joined the Army that following February. Along with 55,000 other Canadian men who would go overseas, it was Vancouver who sent the highest proportion of soldiers to France, higher than any other city on the continent. Half of them would be killed or wounded. Fred serving with the 2nd C.M.R. would be one of them, sent home missing three fingers on his right hand, blown off while loading a cannon. He would never again use a bricklayers trowel.

Alice with the two little girls, Marion and Muriel, and another baby on the way, had a tough time making ends meet. A soldier's pay was not much. According to his pay book, one dollar a day and an additional ten cents for field allowance was all Will made. At Christmas he would fare a little better receiving a total of $95 in December. His pay was sent home to Alice, who was terribly distressed that her husband had gone off to war leaving her in such dire straits. She was not alone. Many Vancouver wives were in similar circumstances. She did manage to earn some money sewing, embroidering and creating one of a kind hats for wealthy Vancouver matrons. But with two little daughters to look after she didn't have a lot of spare time.

In October of 1916 Alice gave birth to a son, Leslie William born at home while his father was far away in France with the 239th Regiment. The Battle of the Somme was raging. This was Britain's most sobering experience in her long military career. Tanks were used for the first time, but they only were capable of doing three miles per hour. Most Canadians who had joined up still had relatives in Britain and figured it would be a chance to "go home" for a visit, do a little fighting and then return home unscathed. It was not to be. The horrors of trench warfare were unspeakable.

Hand dug in a zig-zag fashion by the weary men, the trenches were required to be be seven feet deep, three feet wide at the top and two feet six inches wide at the bottom. The digging usually was done after dusk, but often it was in daylight under the watchful eye and constant shelling of the enemy. Because of the chalk subsoil along the Somme, digging was difficult. When one had dug about three feet down, the rest was solid chalk that had to be pick-axed out. Time spent in these slits of earth often little more than ditches, waiting for the command to go over the top was sickening. Besides the cold, mud and accompanying filth, there were rats and fleas to contend with. The sick, wounded and dead were all about, and the cries of comrades dying beyond the trenches in stretches known as no-man's land rang in your ears day and night. To quote from one soldiers description of the first days battle of the Somme after they went over the top: *"Keeping in line, in extended order, men began to fall one by one. Our officer said we were all right; all the machine guns were firing over our heads. Then the machine guns began the slaughter. Men fell on every side screaming- those who weren't wounded dare not attend to them; we must press on regardless. Hundreds lay on the German barbed-wire, which was not all destroyed. Their bodies formed a bridge for others to pass over and into the German front line."* The battle degenerated to slaughter as the morning progressed.

That opening day of the battle of the Somme, July 1, 1916 ended with 56,000 casualties for the British, from which 21,000 were killed and 35,000 wounded while 600 were taken prisoners by the Germans. The loss on that first day of the Somme easily exceeds the combined casualties of the Crimean War, the Boer War and the Korean War. But this was just the beginning. By autumn the incessant rains had turned the battlefield into a swamp in which tanks being used for the first time and capable at best of doing three miles per hour could not manoeuvre. Sir Douglas Haig, controversial commander of the expeditionary forces thought that one more push would open the road to Bapaume and so costly attacks continued with the attackers often up to their knees in mud. The wounded often drowned, supplies didn't reach the front anymore and guns couldn't get forward. In front of the Butte de Warlencourt, an ancient burial mound, still 3 miles short of Bapaume, the attack finally bogged down. The Canadians had lost 24,029 lives for only a few thousand yards of valueless turf.

The Germans retreated to the Hindenburg line in 1917 leaving the Butte de Warlencourt and Bapaume as a gift to the British side, showing them the futility of their suicide attacks for a few acres of shell pocked ground. The war would return twice to the Somme. But in the memories of Will and the other soldiers who lived through it, the horrors would revisit time and again.

Along with the record of pay, Will's Canadian Soldiers pay-book contained the following information: *"If you are taken prisoner be sure to send a letter or postcard to the Canadian Record Office, giving your address, and any other particulars which are allowed to be written."* I'll bet that was cause for comfort. With the pay book, and a few personal papers carried close to his heart in the pocket of his uniform, Will had photos of Alice, Marion and Muriel and his new baby son Leslie. A letter with pressed violets inside it was addressed to "dear Daddy", fresh violets picked by Marion and Muriel this morning for you. And in childish printing the names Marion, and Muriel along with x's and o's for love and kisses. For her fifth birthday, he managed to send a beautiful little blue and silver pendant necklace home "to my dear little Marion wishing you lots of pretty things on your birthday, with love from your Da da". On the accompanying handmade card he'd drawn her picture.

At one point he got to Paris, and was able to send a fabulous hat home to Alice. She had her picture taken in it and kept it carefully as it was "too special to wear". He often sent tender notes home bearing pencil sketches of areas he'd passed through in the French countryside, extolling the beauties of an abandoned apple orchard, a mill-side pond or fields of lavender. To wile away long hours in the trenches, Will hand-crafted little ships and even a biplane with moveable propeller from scraps of shrapnel or spent bullets. A container for wooden matches was made from a bullet and a curved piece of metal on which he'd etched with a steady hand the word Somme on one side and

Bapaume on the other. He also wove a small basket from river-reeds and made a rather elegant letter-opener with a spent bullet for a handle. Amidst the horrors of war, he was able to take something meant for destruction, re-crafting it into something of use.

On 15 days English leave in September 1918, Will visited with his family in Lifton, Devon and in Cornwall, and with Alice's mother in Plymouth. Despite the hardships everyone was enduring, these visits brought great happiness as he told all about his little daughters, Marion with the dark hair and solemn brown eyes and Muriel, so fair haired and blue eyed. Baby Leslie of course he himself had not yet seen. He extolled the beauties of far away Vancouver where the heavy green forests marched to the very ocean's edge and the mountains rising from the clear blue-green sea seemed never to stop 'til they touched the heavens above.

Will's sister Matilda *(Til)* was so taken by his stories on Vancouver, she decided to move there at the end of the war with her two little boys Gwynn and Mervyn. Her husband Leonard Moore, a young Welshman in the army had been killed and now newly-widowed she was wondering what to do and how to best provide for her young sons. Vancouver seemed the answer where she'd be near her two brothers, Fred and Will and their families.

His leave at an end, Will rejoined his battalion as they slogged ahead from Valenciennes to the Belgian city of Mons which the Germans had occupied for over 4 years. By now everyone had heard rumors that an armistice was in the offing, but as the men reached the city's outskirts they met severe resistance. The Germans were in every house. However, by the night of November 10 the Canadians advanced unapprehended into the centre of the city. The Germans had pulled out. All was eerily quiet. No more sounds of falling bombs, no drone of planes, no rattle of machine guns or rifle shots. And then the residents started streaming into the streets to greet the Canadian soldiers. Other soldiers poured into the city and an honor guard 1,500 strong assembled at the Grand Place. Canadian General Arthur Currie then rode into Mons with an escort of the British 5th Lancers who had fought at the first battle of Mons four years earlier. Currie recorded the event thus: "After doing three cheers for the Belgian King and Queen, and the people, our troops marched to the tune of the Belgian National Anthem, and the thousands in the square sang it, and it was most inspiring." A plaque was later put up by the people. It's inscription reads: *"Mons was captured by the Canadian Corps, on 11th November, 1918. After 50 months of German occupation, freedom was restored to the city. Here was fired the last shot of the Great War."* To paraphrase Irving Berlin's popular World War 1 tune, it was Over Over There!

It would take awhile before the soldiers would once again be home to further celebrations of welcome in Vancouver. Most of them were first sent to camps in England to await passage back to Halifax on ships that were in short supply. In Will's case it was March 23, 1919 before he returned to Canada. After crossing the Atlantic on the S.S. Cretic, of which one of the meals consisted of Lambs Head Broth, Grilled Butterfish, Ox Tail Jardiniere and mashed potatoes, the soldiers traveled across Canada on trains. At every stop there were celebrations to welcome them home and they were handed letters of thanks such as one from the Great War Next Of Kin Association of Medicine Hat which said, "we appreciate the noble deeds of valour performed by our soldiers, who, by their splendid conduct, have brought everlasting honour to themselves and our fair Dominion." It was signed by Mrs. J. McCully, convenor of the train committee. In Moncton, New Brunswick, the Mayor's greetings began with, "Welcome Home! Sons of Canada whether by birth or adoption, welcome home!" It went on to say "You are among those of Canada's heroes to be formally demobilized. We welcome you home to the land of the Maple Leaf! We hail you as the advance guard of Canada's champions of liberty and civilization!"

A poem by Pauline Johnson was addressed to the heroes,

> *Few of you have the blood of kings,*
> *And few are of courtly birth;*
> *But none are vagabonds or rogues*
> *Of doubtful name and worth;*
> *And each has one credential*
> *Which entitles him to brag:*
> *You fought for Right and Canada,*
> *And upheld the British Flag.*

This was all pretty heady stuff.

Chapter 6

No Place Like Home

Upon reaching Vancouver, a huge welcome awaited the returned soldiers. The story of Will's homecoming always made me chuckle. The family was dressed in their very best outfits and excitement rippled through the air. A friend, Alderman Gibbons, owned a touring car *(convertible)* and had offered to take them to the train station to meet and pick up Will.

After the initial thrill of seeing Daddy again, everybody piled into the car. Including the alderman, his wife, Alice, Marion, Muriel, Leslie, and Alice's brother Jack and wife, there were nine of them. There was no seat for the conquering hero! And so Will had to stand on the running board of the car and try and perch on the side of the back door. Marion thought that was just terrible, after he'd been away all those years in the horrid war and now finally home had no place to sit. But she said her Daddy didn't seem to care and waved, cheered and blew kisses to everybody along the way.

Once back home however, it was not easy. Men just off the battlefields were expected to pick up the pieces of their former civilian life and carry on. During the winter of 1918-1919 a world wide epidemic known as the Spanish Flu killed more people than the war itself. As the boys came marching home down the main streets of western cities and towns many in the cheering crowds wore gauze masks in an effort to protect themselves from germs. Fortunately the Phillifant family did not fall victim to the sickness.

There was still not a lot of work available and Will again found himself looking for a way to make a living. To make things worse, for a long time he suffered from terrible nightmares, waking and frightening the entire family. These were the days when post traumatic stress syndrome was unheard of and untreated. Soldiers newly returned from the battlefields were expected to pick up and carry on. What's more, Will felt his place in the family had been usurped by Alice's brother Jack who had more or less acted as a father figure during his absence. His young son Leslie would have little to do with him having bonded with Uncle Jack and Muriel too appeared distant and somewhat wary. Marion however, was thrilled to have her beloved daddy back home and became his best companion, always by his side as he gardened, took walks along the nearby beaches of Burrard Inlet, puttered in his workshop, or entertained her with stories about the war. For a time he had her believing his cleft chin had been caused by a Jerry's bullet.

Greater Vancouver Peace Celebrations were taking place in July of 1919, like one at Hastings Park where all the school children sat in the grandstands and came down a row at a time to receive bronze commemorative medals from Mayor R.H. Gale. They all had to wear red, white or blue tops and marched out to form a huge Union Jack. In Marion's words, "we were all so proud and happy that most of us now had our Dad's home even though some had been terribly scarred. Everyone was trying hard to forget and return to the way things had been before the war, but it was difficult to pick up and carry on as if it had just been a blip." In the poet Wordsworth's words, *Where is it now, the glory and the dream?*

One neighborhood event that wasn't to be missed was the annual Christmas Party given by James Inglis Reid and his wife. He owned a meat market and bakery in downtown Vancouver on Granville Street. His children went to the same school and church *(at that time)* that Marion, Muriel and Leslie attended. The Reids were very generous people and annually held the party for mothers and children on their street. A huge Christmas tree loaded with gifts for all the children and wonderful fancy food heaped on tables made the day magical. The Reids, from Scotland eventually moved out of Grandview to a home near UBC. But for many years Alice continued to loyally shop at his market where the motto was, "We hae meat, that ye can eat, so let the Lord be thank it".

With over one third of Vancouver's population at this time being British, places like Cedar Cove where the Phillifants lived mirrored a community lifted from an English town. Many of Will and Alice's friends from their old home towns in England had now come to Canada and settled nearby. There were the Hawksworths, the Peans, the Rheads and the Clarke's. They visited back and forth. Alice who was an excellent seamstress did lots of sewing, creating drapes, quilts, and entire outfits for people, often accepting some fabric in exchange for her work. Then she would get busy at the Singer treadle sewing machine her mother had shipped from England to her daughter in "the Canadian wilderness", making clothes for her own family from the bartered cloth. And that was how her two little girls were able to be beautifully dressed throughout the lean years. One of the jokes in the family was that thrifty Alice often had just enough of a certain fabric left over to make a matching outfit for Leslie. He was teased unmercifully by other little kids for some of the clothes he wore and called Candlestick when she'd fashioned a matching wine colored velvet hat with tassel for him.

Will, in the meantime, did whatever he could to make ends meet. Clever and inventive at woodworking he built pieces of furniture for people, often from a drawing, or first looking at a fine piece of cabinetry and copying it. For a time he worked at Wallace Shipyards *(Burrard Dry-dock)* in North Vancouver where the Princess Louise was being built for the Canadian Pacific. Touted as an all

B.C. product, when the ship was launched, 9 year old Marion whose second name was Louise proudly accompanied her father to the ceremonies. Eventually he worked at the Restmore Furniture Company on Clark Drive and Venables. One of their large billboards pictured a white bearded Rip Van Winkle, and declared, "If Rip Van Winkle had used his head, he'd have slept 20 years on a Restmore bed". Will put his talents to use at that company where, one of his specialties was french polishing. Inlays, fretwork, beading and hand crafted brass drawer pulls were also favorites. He made most of their household furniture. However, when the wolf was at the door select pieces had to be sold to put food on the table.

Chapter 7

A Place With Potential

Alice had always wanted to move up the hill, away from the waterfront where it was often cold and damp. Throughout the fall and winter the mists often hung heavily over Burrard Inlet and trying to keep warm and dry were problems. It was also a long walk for Marion and Muriel who were attending Hastings School. Em and Fred Phillifant, now living in a new house on Parker Street, just off Templeton Drive came up with an idea. A house on Venables Street, just across the back lane from them was for sale. Indeed it had stood empty for sometime and was referred to as "the old haunted house". Not a single windowpane remained unbroken, and the three story structure needed plenty of work. It was truly a fixer-upper, but with possibilities. Em agreed to purchase it and then Alice and Will would pay her back at so much per month. A deal was struck. The wooden house with it's hip roof and large front verandah, was bought for $2,200.

Will went to work repairing and refurbishing to make it livable. Alice's brother Jack helped, drawing on his skills as a painter/plasterer. Thanks to Will's ability to scavenge such things as slabs of grey marble from a demolished Vancouver hotel washroom, which he made into pantry counter tops and his way with finishing touches on wooden banister rails and window moldings, and the reconstruction of a beautiful corner fireplace with leaf green hand-painted tiles from Holland the place soon emerged as a proper home. There was a basement, main floor, top floor and an attic with small balcony. The lot was a good size, and over the years he spent hours happily building cut stone retaining walls at the front of the property and transforming the overgrown yard into gardens. A fishpond, stone birdbath, and rose trellised pathway leading from the flower garden to the vegetable patch would be bordered at the fence by raspberry canes. A single car garage near the back lane never would hold an automobile, but it's walls provided a sturdy place to yearly string fragrant sweetpeas while bolstering mounds of pink honeysuckle.

Beneath the back porch, which eventually Will glassed in with odds and ends of sometimes murky panes, was his potting area with worn brick floors, and bench areas holding clutches of clay pots, seedlings and potting mixtures. As a little kid I loved going in there and pretending it was my playhouse. It was one place I could spray water and mix mud-pies to my hearts content. Nobody seemed to mind the mess. And if I peered through the imperfect glass at people and things outside it was a bit like being in the house of mirrors at the P.N.E. where heads and bodies didn't always line up.

The basement became Will's workshop where he was forever creating things, like an ill-fated incubator for his chickens. It seems he decided to try using part of Alice's new wringer washer in the incorporation of this invention. He probably hooked something up to the motor. Whatever the plan it was not terribly successful and the poor hatchlings were cremated on the spot. To make matters worse, the washing machine wouldn't work again.

The family had not inhabited the house long when Marion became ill with smallpox and the place was quarantined. Alice and Marion stayed inside, but Will had to work, so stayed with his sister while Muriel and Leslie were sent to their Auntie Em's for the duration. Once the quarantine had been lifted and everyone allowed back home, only one day passed before little Muriel developed Scarlet Fever, followed by young Leslie. Alice was quarantined again with her brood. She nursed the three children through these terrible diseases and must have been utterly exhausted. They all made it through unscathed except for Marion who lost the hearing in one ear after her ordeal.

Jack *(Uncle)* had lost his wife Helen *(Sis)* to T.B. in 1920. She was 42 years old. They had been married fifteen years, a childless marriage during which she was plagued with ill health. She was interred at Ocean View Cemetery where for the rest of his life he would travel by streetcars or buses once a month to put fresh flowers on her grave. He was now left alone in the house they'd shared on Eton Street. After a year of working, coming home to an empty place and having to cook for himself, or eat at one of his sister's place's, it was decided he would rent out his house and move in with Will and Alice's family on Venables Street, an arrangement deemed sensible for all concerned. A large upstairs back bedroom became his, and he was given a corner of the dining room for his easy chair, lamp, end table and radio. This was his domain, where he smoked his pipe and listened to classical music, as he read from his week's supply of library books, the popular magazine, Saturday Evening Post, or Punch.

Once Uncle had moved in, the financial situation improved. He paid for piano lessons with Professor John Borthwick for Marion and Muriel, and eventually also singing lessons for Marion and Leslie after they'd given up on piano. He saw to it that they received lots of books for reading and took them to musical events. Up until he died in 1957 at 82, he weekly walked or took the street car or bus downtown to the main library *(Carnegie)* on the corner of Main and Hastings Streets to get his reading material which consisted of three or four books. He never wore glasses and had perfect vision. Thursday nights he would attend church choir practice where he was librarian and sang in the choir. Sunday mornings he always attended Grandview United and most Sunday evenings he traveled by streetcar downtown to Christ Church Cathedral for Evensong. In season he attended cricket or soccer matches at nearby parks and if a good English comedy was being shown at a downtown movie theatre, he'd be sure to attend. Movies like The Bells of St. Trinians were his favorites. He had a dry wit.

With Grandview United Church *(now the Vancouver East Cultural Center)* sitting on the corner of Victoria Drive and Venables Street just three blocks from the Phillifant's home, the entire family was very involved in all aspects of church life. Indeed it became their second home. For a time the church had been known as Grandview Methodist, built when members of the Princess Street Methodist *(a small frame church on Park Drive)* outgrew their facilities. One of it's first ministers was the Rev. F.G. Lett *(father of Chief Justice Sherwood Lett)*.

Will was always working on something down at the church and whenever they needed something built, he was one of the first to be asked. He made the communion table, the pedestal plant stands, the hymn boards, and various other pieces. But his crowning fete was the building of a bowling alley in the church hall basement partly so the A.O.T.S. *(men's service group whose initials stood for As One That Serves)*, of which he was a member could bowl each week.

Grandview was booming. It was now the city's most populous area. The church had attracted a huge congregation of over 800. Besides the church building with Sunday School classes in it's basement, and manse next door where the minister and his family lived, the complex included tennis courts on the Victoria Drive corner, and across the back lane, fronting on Adanac Street, the large church hall with a stage. The bowling alley was beneath this hall and the Beginner's Department of the Sunday School department next to it. A caretakers house where the Bert Turner family resided was perched behind the church, resembling an overgrown playhouse. As a kid I often wondered how adults could actually live in such a tiny house. With a little spiral staircase going to the one upstairs bedroom, it resembled a lighthouse. Bert was a happy, elfin-like man, one of many war-wounded in that congregation, he'd been a regimental sergeant major, left with pieces of shrapnel embedded in his legs. Every once in awhile a piece would work its way out and he'd be sitting in the tenor section of the choir loft, with a pool of blood at his feet. He'd limp out aided by his wife Ethel. In all the time I knew him, *(he was caretaker at Grandview United for 39 years)* he never complained or admitted to having a bad day. He was a dear friend of Will's and of Jack's. He wrote a short poem called Armistice which in 1930 he penned in Marion's autograph album. "Over the broken dead, over the trenches and wire, Bugles of God rang out - cease fire. Woe to those nations of men who in their heat of desire, Break that stern order of God - Cease Fire!" Perhaps a bit oppressive for a young girl's collection.

There was something going on at Grandview all the time. Morning and evening services, choir practice, Sunday school, orchestra, tennis, badminton, bowling, CGIT, women's groups like WA, Friendship Circle, and men's groups like the AOTS as well as a huge Young People's Organization and at the other end of the scale called The Baby Band. Alice was always cooking, baking or sewing for some function at the church, preferring to remain on the sidelines as a quiet doer.

One of Alice's little frustrations was the fact that Will was consistently late for the 11 o'clock Sunday church service. He would dawdle around until it was time for her, the three children and Uncle to head out the door to walk the three blocks down Venables to Victoria Drive. As they went out the door, he went upstairs to put his tie and jacket on. When all were nicely seated in their pew, the choir had processed in and the first hymn was being sung, in would walk Will smiling and nodding his good morning's as he made his way down the aisle. He did this his whole life. Marion once said he was probably always late because it wasn't until everyone had gotten out of the house that he finally had a chance to use the one bathroom.

These were the days of the annual Sunday School Picnics on Union Steamship's SS Lady Alexandra to Belcarra Park or Bowen Island. Young People's Groups travelled by boat to summer camps at far-off spots like Sechelt on the Sunshine Coast. Musical events and plays were constantly going on at the church hall, and huge Christmas concerts took place. Easter cantatas drew people from all over the city. There would often be massed choirs singing Handel's Messiah and the church would be decorated with hundreds of lilies and palms. There was even a church orchestra. The names of church members read like a who's who list of the day. Odlums, Letts, Avisons, Fullertons and so on.

The Phillifant children now attended Lord Nelson School where one day enroute to school Marion was knocked down and run over by a horse and buggy. Despite a lengthy convalescence, for bed-rest was the considered treatment of the day, she was plagued with back problems after. Having missed so much school that term she was held back a year while her sister Muriel who was a bit of a whiz at school, was put forward a year. This meant they ended up in the same classroom, which didn't work out at all. The problem was solved when Marion changed over to King Edward High School, preferring lengthy streetcar rides rather than compete with her sister. Muriel and eventually Leslie attended and graduated from Britannia High School between Woodland and Cotton Drives.

In the fall of 1929 the Wall Street Market began to decline, and then broke. Because the city of Vancouver was economically dependent on the export of lumber, salmon, wheat and minerals when the bottom fell out of the market the number of jobless soared. June of that year however had seen a happy event in the wedding of Em and Fred Phillifant's daughter Elsie to Fred Drane. Reminiscent of the era, the wedding party of which Marion and Muriel were bridesmaids, wore short dresses and Marion's hair beneath a picture hat, was bobbed! She had defied her father by getting her lovely long dark hair cropped; something he never quite got over.

The oldest pioneering building in Vancouver, Hastings Mill, closed down on Burrard Inlet just east of Main. Slated for demolition, it was given a last minute reprieve when the Native Daughters of B.C. *(nothing to do with today's "natives")* paid to have it removed from it's stilts and floated by barge to a new location at the north end of Alma Street. Will was there along with a host of other pioneers to see it leave it's original pilings and to recall memories of picking up supplies there at the early part of the century. The old mill saw new life as The Museum of B.C. Historical Relics where it can be visited to this day in tree shaded Pioneer Park. The cookhouse bell that so long ago signalled the arrival of the Royal Mail has been preserved along with a host of other interesting relics. As a kid I remember visiting the museum and playing the old harpsichord that came "Round the Horn".

The first talkies had arrived at theatres by 1930 with films such as All Quiet on the Western Front starring Lew Ayres, while Ronald Coleman and Loretta Young headlined a movie called The Devil To Pay. People were singing songs like "I'll Get By As Long As I Have You", and "I Don't Know Why I Love You Like I Do." These and other toe-tapping melodies could be heard from the Panorama Roof of the Hotel Vancouver where Mart Kenney and his Western Gentlemen, Canadas' favorite Big Band were broadcasting nightly. Their theme song, The West, A Nest and You was so popular it almost became a sort of national anthem for the country. From coast to coast people tuned their radios in to listen or dance to his soothing strains.

In 1931, Emma Warne *(Alice, Jack and Em's mother)* died. A letter edged in black arrived at the Phillifant home, along with a letter written by their brother Alf in which he noted, "She has gained the peace she earned, which we may all get, but do not deserve." A small program of her funeral service, a card of silver and black bearing a picture of a single white rose was enclosed. Buried in the Old Cemetery, Plymouth, she was seventy-seven. Sadly, she had never seen her beloved Canadian grandchildren other than in photographs and only knew them through the letters they wrote "to dear Grandma" each month telling her what they were up to. She had worked very hard her entire life, never had much money, but managed always to send interesting packages to the children containing beautiful little things she had made.

Marion was working at Spencer's Department Store on West Hastings and Richards Streets. It had opened just a year before designed by the same architects *(McCarter and Nairne)* as the Marine Building. Spencer's, a general type department store sold most everything a person could want at that time. A glass arcade on the Hastings Street side of the store featured especially beautiful displays at Easter with lavish plantings of fresh spring flowers, ponds, fountains, arched bridges, and baby chicks and bunnies. At Christmas the arcade was turned into a magical snow-filled landscape or perhaps an animated Santa's workshop while the carols of Christmas hung on the air both inside and outside the store. June was when they did their wedding window and the entire block of the glass arcade would be transformed into a churches aisle with all the wedding party mannequins in the popular attire of that year. People travelled to town just to view the arcade, lining up eagerly, faces pressed to the plate glass. But another of the department store's innovations lay on the top floor of the store and was called... The Party Shop! This is where Marion found her niche.

Odd as it may seem, while the depression was beginning, the wealthy of Vancouver were able to "play" more. This was the era of extravagant dinner parties and social events. Everyone in the upper echelons of Vancouver society was trying to outdo each other. The newspapers social pages were full of lengthy descriptions of gala events.

Marion had come into her own. She often told me about certain "upper crust" types coming into the store perhaps with their chauffeur to carry purchases, and asking for some wild idea for a table centerpiece and party favors. She could always come up with something wonderful. Crepe paper was in favor at this time and she would spend hours crafting a giant swan or sea shell covered in the paper petals as a receptacle to hold fresh flowers on a client's table. Other times she'd make multiple paper roses to cover archways for a lavish wedding, or perhaps giant Christmas crackers to travel end to end on someone's banquet table. For all of this she was paid two dollars a day and worked more than eight hours most days *(with no overtime pay)* six days a week. She even had to box the creations, and ride the freight elevator to the basement floor for the limousines and their accompanying servants to pick up the orders. After work she took a streetcar on Hastings up as far as Commercial Drive and Venables, then trudged up that hill to home in the 2100 block. It made for a long day followed by warmed up supper, for the rest of the family had always eaten by 5 p.m.. For the two weeks leading up to Christmas employees had to be at work an hour early in order to sing in the Spencer's Department Store Choir which went out over the radio before opening time.

By 1932 the new airport at Sea Island and the Burrard Street Bridge had opened. But hundreds of unemployed men rode the freights to Vancouver where winters were milder. Hobo jungles sprung up and there were frequent clashes between demonstrators and police. Brother Can You Spare A Dime, made popular by crooner Bing Crosby that year became the theme song of The Depression. For anyone who had the money, Woodward's was advertising women's shoes for $2.45 a pair and the Bay had a special on men's blazers and flannels. Seven dollars would get you both items. New York boneless steaks were advertised for 20 cents a pound. But who could afford steak?

Chapter 8

Enter The Cupits

Many men lucky enough to be employed were only working a few hours per day. One of these was young Arthur Cupit who worked for his Uncle Tom Davies in his plumbing and sheet metal shop at 1941 Commercial Drive where the sign painted on the window said "Sanitary Work a Specialty." The wooden sidewalk in front of the shop usually had a cast iron bathtub on display. Art often had to take a hot water tank, tub or toilet on the streetcar or tram to his job. He used to joke that if it was a toilet delivery at least he had a seat.

Art had been born in Aston, near Liverpool, County of Lancashire England, November, 1905, the second son of Grace and Harry Cupit. With his older brother Jack, younger brother's Frank and Ernie *(also born in Lancashire)* and sister Lillian, born in Vancouver, the family lived on the corner of McLean Drive and Graveley Street in a near new wooden two-storey home with basement that their bricklayer father had proudly purchased around 1914. From the front verandah there was at that time a pleasant view of False Creek Flats which lay just a block downhill from them to the west on Clark Drive, while to the north The Lions in all their regalness often crowned with snow could be enjoyed from the dining room or kitchen pantry windows. It was a pleasant middle-class district of predominantly English immigrants.

The family *(except for father Harry)* attended Grandview United Church where the brothers played in the Sunday School orchestra and, along with their little sister as they grew, took advantage of the tennis courts and bowling alley.

Most everyone in Grandview knew three of the Cupit brothers, but Art was the quiet one often mistakenly thought to just be one of their friends instead of the fourth brother. He had gone to work at age 15 to assist the family, his paycheck helping put two of his brother's and sister through university. Working for his Uncle Tom was no picnic. He was a dour bible-thumping Baptist that believed hard work and little pay built character. He was married to Art's mother's sister, Mary a quiet lovely lady. They lived above the family business on Commercial Drive where Uncle Tom kept a whistle which he blew at the bottom of the stairs leading to their apartment in order to notify Mary that he'd soon be up for his noon meal. They had three children, Margaret, Mabel and George, one daughter Eveline having died at age nine.

Henry Herbert *(Harry)* Cupit had emigrated to Canada in 1911 the same year two of his brothers also left England, one going to Australia and the other to Boston, Massachusetts. In Vancouver Harry boarded for a time with Mary and Tom Davies, leaving wife Grace and their four sons in Liverpool until he could get enough money ahead to forward their passage.

Harry had been born in the county of Lancashire to William Cupit, a corn miller from Crofton, Lincoln, and his wife Ann *(nee Bailey)* born in Scredington, Lincoln. William and Ann had been married in 1860 at St. Peter's Church, Liverpool where most of their offspring were also christened. Not much is known of Harry's childhood, other than the fact it was not a very happy one. The youngest in the family, he had six brothers and one sister all born in

Liverpool. The eldest brother Ambrose, was 18 years older than Harry. It is believed their mother died when Harry was about two and their father remarried. Brought up by a stepmother who it seems treated him poorly, Harry was sent to work in a factory at a very young age *(9 yrs)* under terrible conditions. He refused to talk much about those early years or his siblings. It seems he had some kind of religious upbringing *(whether negative or not)* for his little catechism book still exists along with a couple of certificates bearing his name from a Methodist Sunday School he attended in Birmingham. And although he was not a church goer, he did believe in God. Perhaps his leanings were towards Calvinism for he had several books including "Under Calvin's Fury" on his shelf.

Chapter 9

The St. Ives Connection

Grace, was one of seven children born to John and Elizabeth Renowden of St. Ives, Cornwall. Wesleyan Methodists, their father often preached at services. John, who had first worked as a tin dresser and later as an insurance agent in a definite switch of careers, had been born in Walstetown, St. Ives and had married Elizabeth Ann *(Beckerleg)* of Marazion, Cornwall in 1870. Elizabeth was the daughter of Thomas Pearce Beckerleg, a blacksmith and Ellen *(nee Quine)* Beckerleg. The seven children born to Elizabeth and John were Nancy, John, Elizabeth, Mary and William John *(who died at 18 months)*, Grace, and William Edward.

Elizabeth died *(probably in childbirth)* in 1880 and John Renowden remarried in 1881 to Sara. Three more children, Robert, Mabel and Lucy were born to them.

The Renowden name interestingly can be traced back to a family "de Trenode" in Cornwall from the 12th century. By the 15th century the name spelled Renoden can be found in Bodmin and Penwith and in 1452 the priest in the parish of Mylor was a John Renowden. There are records of two monks ordained about that time. While the Bodmin branch sometimes spelled the name Renorden, they died out by the end of the 17th century. However the West Penwith branch of the family continues to thrive today with a strong group around Penzance. One branch in St. Hilary began to experiment with the spelling of the name inventing the Trenowden variation early in the 19th century. It was about this time when the bulk of the Cornish adopted the Renowden spelling.

Myths and folklore abound in Cornwall, that toe-shaped tip of England on the Atlantic Ocean where from the edge of Bodmin Moors to Penzance and Lands End, lie ancient emerald pastures punctuated by hostile rocky cliffs and coves; terrain made famous by Daphne DuMaurier's novels. Grace often talked about the old festivals such as the Flurry Dance where men in top hats wreathed with flowers and women and children in white paraded through the street to welcome spring. Her hometown of St. Ives is to this day a charming cobblestone streeted fishing village surrounded on three sides by sunny beaches. Legends teem in Cornwall where the ruins of Tintagel Castle, reported birthplace of King Arthur, still stand and Merlin's cave, carved out of the cliffs by restless waves rests on the beach below. Elizabeth, Grace's mother, came from Marazion where one of the most spectacularly situated castles, St. Michael's Mont stands. The spirits of the Celts are said to haunt the mystic stone circles and altars left from a previous age perhaps resting uneasily because Cornwall was the first of the modern Celtic nations to lose it's language. Whether Grace knew any Cornish other than "deth da" which means hello, is hard to say, but her love for Cornwall and her many relatives there never diminished.

At about five feet, six inches in height, Grace, born March 9, 1878 at St. Ives, was a quiet soft-spoken person, her brown eyes framed with dark brows and hair. She played the piano and with her sisters, sang in the church choir. After marrying handsome blue-eyed, blond-haired Harry *(who was about 5'4' in height)*, on February 7, 1903 at Belmont Row Wesleyan Chapel in Aston, she soon found herself with a large family of four lively boys to look after while her husband was often away working as a bricklayer or stone mason on jobs in other areas of England. They resided in an austere brick Liverpool row house in a district called Old Swan, a far cry from her girlhood country home in St. Ives, with it's hollyhock bordered gardens and fresh Atlantic breezes.

Graces' sister Mary and husband Tom Davies had emigrated to Vancouver in September 1909 and were doing very well. It is quite likely they sent reports home on the glowing economy and it didn't take much to persuade Harry to take a chance on a new and better life for his young family in a growing city of opportunity being marketed by realtors as "The Liverpool of the Pacific." One in three people in Vancouver were of British birth at this time. And so he had gone on ahead, working at his trade as a bricklayer while saving money to bring his wife and four boys to the Pacific coast.

As a youngster of four or five, Arthur had nearly died from an abcess on one of his lungs. Hospitalized in Liverpool, he was operated on in a rather primitive method in which they removed some ribs leaving him with a large unsightly scar and permanent indentation in his back. They had however saved his life.

In 1912 Harry had finally been able to send for Grace, and along with the barest of possessions she and the children from 6 month old Ernie to 9 year old Jack sailed from Liverpool on the Allan Line's Virginian, the same ship that had brought Alice Warne to Canada just a year earlier. Now it was April, the same week the ill-fated Titanic was on the Atlantic and the distress calls from that ship were heard by those on-board where at 6:00 a.m. a wireless message from the Virginian to the Californian, also in the vicinity, asked "Do you know the Titanic has struck a berg and she is sinking?" As the saying goes, the rest is history. The tragedy of the sinking of the Titanic and fact Grace and her young sons had been on the sea at the same time was something she never forgot.

Upon arrival in Montreal, Grace had to keep her youngsters in line as they began the long train trip across Canada to Vancouver.

How she coped with minding four eager children on a trip like that boggles the mind. At one point her eldest son Jack, always the inquisitive one, vanished for a time and there was much concern that perhaps he'd gotten off the train at a prior stop. Luckily, he eventually showed up, having just taken a stroll to another train car. Like many pioneers before her, Grace made it safely to Vancouver, where the family shared accommodations with the Davies above the plumbing and sheet metal shop on Commercial Drive. Instead of separate rooms, they slept dormitory style, each bed separated by a sheet or blanket suspended from the ceiling. When baby Lillian arrived, *(so the story goes)*, she was put in a bed made from a bottom bureau drawer.

By 1915 things were going well for the Cupit family in their McLean Drive house. It was a good time to be settling in bustling Grandview whose central area was now covered in new homes within walking distance of numerous Commercial Drive shops. It had the feeling of a distinct little village. And along Grandview's shoreline new industrial plants and port facilities had sprung up.

Harry had lots of work as brick buildings jockeyed for position on young Vancouver's city skyline. A good bricklayer, he worked for Dominion Construction on such projects as the *(now demolished)* Georgia Medical Dental Building, the Marine Building, the Rogers Building at Pender and Granville and the Great Northern Train Station on Main Street, as well as various schools, hospitals, hotels and smaller buildings. In the West Kootenay he worked on the beautiful courthouse in Nelson. At times when there wasn't a project in B.C., Harry worked across the border in Tacoma or Seattle, Washington where he helped build the Smith Tower. This was often done in the busy building days with crews from Washington sometimes working on B.C. structures. The men went where the work was in those days, leaving their families to run the home base in their absence. In 1921 the sixth census of Canada showed bricklayers, masons and stonecutters averaging $973.82 annual earnings.

The Cupit's upbringing was strict. Harry, ruled with an iron fist, keeping a leather strap hanging from his chair at the dinner table. Whether he used it often we don't know, but he used to boast he had only to touch it in order to regain control of his boys. Lily, as he fondly called Lillian, could do no wrong. With her long blonde hair and pretty blue eyes she was her father's pride and joy. Although Arthur was the introspective child of the family, he had a mischievous streak and often was dismissed from the table and sent to bed by his father with no dinner. Then his mother, ever the soft-hearted girl from Cornwall, would manage to smuggle some supper to him at a later hour.

Art was the boy who gave his older brother Jack a hot foot by lighting matches between his toes while he slept. And he was the innocent looking lad who backed up to the oven door, pulled all the center from a fresh baked loaf of bread, all the while smiling sweetly and saying, "I'm not doing anything Momma." She said he had the most beautiful deep blue eyes fringed with dark lashes.

The Cupit boys enjoyed skating in winter on frozen False Creek before setting off for Grandview School which was located on 1st Avenue between Cotton and Commercial Drive. They had a little black and white dog, and various cats including a huge Persian named Fluffy. Jack had an after-school job and Art had a morning route delivering The World, Vancouver's daily newspaper with offices out of what later became The Sun Tower on the corner of Beatty and Pender Streets. His route was quite a large one, and he had to deliver one paper to the forboding looking Immigration Building with it's barred windows, down near the CPR dock. All the family were musical. Grace played the piano, Harry strummed the mandolin, Jack played the violin, Arthur the saxophone, using a book for his lessons by Ben Vereecken, who was a member of John Phillip Sousa's Band. Frank played the violin and Ernie and Lillian, the piano. If music wasn't filling their household it meant studying was. Harry placed much emphasis on education because he'd had so little.

By 1926 Frank had entered University, Ernie was attending Britannia High School and Lillian was entering 7th grade.

Jack was working away from home now at Buntzen Lake where a huge hydro electric power plant had been built at Ruskin by B.C. Electric. He was planning to wed Marion Schooley, a pretty Grandview girl who lived with her family in a large corner house complete with turret opposite Grandview Park. The Schooley family also attended Grandview United Church. They had suffered a heartbreaking tragedy when their young son *(a newspaper carrier)* had been found murdered under a viaduct.

Although the Cupit home was on the corner of McLean Drive and Graveley Street, a long narrow lot next to it, fronting on Graveley had been purchased by Harry in a tax sale, and this was where Grace had her gardens, vegetable and flower bordered by a row of laburnum *(golden chain)* trees and a beloved lilac with mauve blooms at the foot of her back porch. Of the four similar houses on McLean Drive, named for Vancouver's first Mayor Malcolm McLean, Harry and Grace's home was painted two shades of grey, the one next door in browns and the other two in a hue known as CPR red. It was a color that took years to fade, finally mellowing to an anaemic tomato soup color. Before Harry had purchased the bordering vacant lot all these houses had enjoyed the "borrowed" piece of property. Harry put an end to their communal gardening when he constructed a fence saying "good fences make good neighbors." That adage and "never a lender or borrower be," were two of his favorites.

Sports and more sports kept the Cupit's busy as they grew. Typical kids, they road bikes and played games in the bushes just opposite their house. In snowy weather they rode their wooden sleighs down the steep incline that was Graveley Street. As they grew older, cars, now driving on the right became their passion. Art and Frank built a large square garage near the back lane where they worked on their model A and T Fords. Art also had a small boat that he moored at Coal Harbor. Often he and Frank, and sometimes Ernie would travel to Vancouver Island where in the twenties you could get a full-course lunch at Hudsons Bay for fifty cents. To quench your thirst on a hot day, you could sip a bottle of Whistle. If you wanted something stronger however, you had to first buy a $2.00 permit. The Cupit boys didn't drink alcohol, so such permits weren't a concern. Sometimes they took a trip south of the border, travelling along Bellingham's famed Chuckanut Drive or to B.C.'s interior, following the treacherous Fraser Canyon route. At this time Art was driving a Model T Ford with a canvas roof. It was his pride and joy, but couldn't have been comfortable by today's standards. About 1928 a real innovation hit Vancouver when the first White Spot opened out on South Granville and you could have car hop service for your burger and shake.

Harry Cupit never owned or drove an automobile, so Grace had to walk from McLean Drive up Graveley Street which consisted of three extremely steep hills in order to shop on Commercial Drive. This was an almost daily excursion for her and most other housewives. Meat and other perishables couldn't be kept long in the days before every kitchen had a refrigerator. She'd buy her eggs, cheese and butter at McComber Brothers where in a September 1922 advertisement in the Highland Echo, the local paper, prices for Creamery Butter were 43 cents or 3 pounds for $1.25, B.C. Storage eggs were 40 cents a dozen or three dozen for $1.15, and pullets were 3 dozen for 85 cents. She probably purchased her meat at McCombers too, where the floors behind that counter were covered in sawdust. Other grocery items came from the Piggly Wiggly on the corner of Graveley and Commercial. Milk was delivered daily in glass bottles from the Crystal Dairy by horse drawn wagon as was bread, *(if she didn't bake it herself)* from the 4X Bread Company. Vegetables not grown in one's own garden could be purchased at the door from Wah Lee's old canvas curtained black Ford truck. Fresh fish was delivered intermittently by an old Oriental with a pole strung across his shoulders from which hung two baskets of the days catch. All in all, the need to travel down town was rare, as Commercial Drive from Venables out to Broadway thronged with stores providing all services. Most districts in Vancouver were like individual little villages, each with their own character, and characters!

Grace's relatives, the Davies, had a large summer camp at Crescent Beach a half block from the ocean and family members often went there during the summer months for large get-togethers under the big roofed verandah which had a stone fireplace built into one end; the perfect place to warm up after an evening swim. Especially during the depression years when not much travelling was done, being able to spend time at Crescent was heavenly. There was a gramophone on which to play records and a pump organ in the living room used to accompany family sing-alongs... hymns usually if the Davies were in residence. The Cupit's however tended to be a little more adventurous.

The 30's saw the city of Vancouver hit rock-bottom. The incomplete Second Narrows Bridge lay idle and rusting while the gaunt hulk of the new Hotel Vancouver on which all work had been suspended hung over the city like a cloud of doom as idle men stood around on street corners and beggars went door to door. Breadlines were a common sight as the unemployed shuffled along to soup kitchens like the one set up at First United Church where over 1,250 were regularly being fed. Property was worth nothing with a lot in the East End assessed at $1,500 being advertised for $150 with no takers in sight.

Jack Cupit and Marion Schooley were now married and living at Ruskin where in just the space of a few years they had lost 3 baby sons, born prematurely. Frank Cupit had graduated from University and was teaching in a one-room school at Hedley where in the summers he worked in the nickel plate mine. He had met and soon married dark-haired Marguerite Curry from Oliver, who had been working for the telephone company as a switchboard operator. Only Art, Ernie and Lillian were still at the McLean Drive home with their parents who in 1932 took a trip to England for a visit with relatives. Ernie who had graduated with honors from U.B.C. had begun teaching at Strathcona School where he had 40 children in his class, and Lillian was in her last year of university, planning also to be a school teacher. Although he would never verbalize it, Harry was proud of his offspring.

Sometime in 1933, Art Cupit and Marion Phillifant met at Grandview United Church where she sang in the soprano section of the choir. He was so shy it took him sometime to get up the courage to ask her for a date. He would wait patiently outside the choir room door after Sunday's church service for her to exit. But she always seemed to be accompanied by a boisterous group of friends. They'd walk right past him, chatting away as they headed for somebody's car. And she'd be gone! Outgoing and friendly, Marion was always willing to take a dare, and much to her sister Muriel's consternation had no lack of male attention. When she and Art began dating, no one could believe it. Art, they thought, far too reserved and quiet for Marion. But opposites do attract.

The Phillifant family immediately took to Art, probably thinking he'd be a good steadying influence for Marion, who had been known to be a bit of a flirt. And so the couple began dating in what became a lifelong love affair. Church socials were mainly the entertainment of the day as there wasn't any money to spare. Just savoring an ice cream cone from the Crystal Dairy on Commercial Drive was a big deal. With it's marble counters and floors, large ceiling fans and chairs with one large sized arm just right for resting a frosted glass holding a milk-shake, it was one of Grandview's most popular spots. Marion's favorite flavour was maple walnut, but Art's was always vanilla which she thought totally boring! She'd tease him saying, "be adventurous, try something different", and he'd reply in his quiet way, "but I like vanilla!"

Chapter 10

Baby Face, Vancouver's Own

The depression still hung like a pall over Vancouver, but the newspapers were full of stories of another Grandview boy, Jimmy McLarnin, born in Inchicore, Ireland who with his parents, and 11 brothers and sisters lived in the 1500 block of Williams Street, near Grandview Park. Young Jimmy was nine when the family moved to Vancouver. His father Sam, had been a butcher in Ireland, but in Vancouver they ran a secondhand furniture store down on East Hastings. As a kid, Jimmy hawked newspapers down on the Vancouver docks. But by 1923 he had broken into the limelight of boxings big time, first capturing the welterweight title in Los Angeles on May 29, 1933 when he knocked out Young Corbett. When word of Jimmy's "two minutes and 37 seconds of glory" reached Vancouver that night, movie theatre managers halted their feature presentations to take the stage and announce the news. People went crazy, streaming into the streets and cheering.

Under the tutelage of his trainer and manager, Pop Foster, a Yorkshireman who became his life long mentor and friend, Jimmy had reached celebrity status as Baby Face, the Grandview kid in the emerald green trunks and cape with the golden harp of Ireland emblazoned on it. Touted in the newspapers as "Vancouver's Own,"

Jimmy was also headlined in various sports stories as "the Beltin Celt, the Belfast Bomber, the Murderous Mick and the Dublin Dynamiter! They also called him the Jew Killer, a label he hated. The Irish wanted to see him beat the Jews and the Jewish fans wanted to see him beaten! Baby Face, attesting to his youthful good looks was the moniker most used. Jimmy, with all the media hype and worship from fans 'round the world was completely captivated by a pretty blonde haired girl who first caught his eye as she played tennis at Grandview Park where he did his laps. She was the little sister of the Cupit boys, Lillian.

The day after his lightning kayo in the first round gave him the title, Vancouver's depression-ridden citizens eagerly embraced Jimmy as a great morale booster to their otherwise mundane existence. The Province newspaper acknowledged "Jimmy of Vancouver" saying, Vancouver hadn't known such an hour since Percy Williams won the hundred yards in the Amsterdam Olympics. There were four stories on the front page of The Province that day and a picture of "Baby Face" and his manager. More stories and a picture appeared on the sports page, although no action pictures as this was before wire photos had been invented. Readers were told that some of the famous ringsiders at the fight were Mae West, Bing Crosby, George Raft and Joe E. Brown.

Jimmy, however, was more than Vancouver's favorite son: he was also the toast of Broadway, sharing the sports pages on a regular basis with people like Jack Dempsey and Babe Ruth. He was a friend of New York mayor Jimmy Walker, a golfing partner of Bing Crosby and Bob Hope and often dined or hobnobbed with movie stars like Jean Harlow, Barbara Stanwyck and even Mae West who had invited him to come up and see her sometime. That was an offer he said he didn't take, he was in love with Lillian Cupit.

Upon his return to Vancouver after winning the championship of the world, young Jimmy was greeted by a police band playing Wearing o' the Green at his front door. Riding high on publicity, everyone wanted him for guest of honor. But one of the first things he did was to visit the gym of First United Church where he gave a talk to a group of kids to build up their morale and inspire them to greater things. The pep talk took place beneath a painting of the old rugged cross on one of the walls. Jimmy told how he'd knocked out Young Corbett with a one-two and a right to the jaw. Then he suggested they'd be okay in life if they would always follow through that way. "Remember fellows, don't smoke, don't drink, and don't go around with girls. Read the bible in your spare time and roll with the punches."

Harry Cupit had been anything but keen on the idea of his fair-haired schoolteacher daughter dating, much less marrying a boxer, even if he was a celebrity. But she had looked at no one else since first meeting Jimmy at age sixteen. Several years her senior, riding high on popularity and earning money in amounts only dreamed about by most people at that time, Jimmy was able to shower his beloved with wonderful gifts. Flowers from Vancouver's most elegant downtown florist, chocolates from Victoria's famed Rogers, jewels, furs, French perfume and beautiful clothes all made their way to his darling Lily. Grace with her humble beginnings in Cornwall could scarcely believe the extravagances. Harry didn't know what he should do other than forbid marriage until she had turned twenty-one.

That January of 1935 saw Vancouver's worst winter storm ever recorded when on the 21st more than 43 centimeters (3½ feet) of snow fell with icy gale winds. The roof of the Hastings Street Forum collapsed and there was ice on the Fraser River where crews tried to dynamite passages for boats to get through. But by May when Jack and Marion Cupit welcomed a baby daughter, Marilyn Shirley, the first grandchild for Grace and Harry, winter's wrath had been forgotten. Plans for Lillian's marriage to Jimmy were also being finalized. With so much publicity always following everything Jimmy did, and not wanting the wedding to be a public affair, the decision was made to hold the ceremony at the Cupit home instead of a church. They would try to keep the July date a secret from the press. However a story appeared in the Province with huge headlines stating *McLarnin to wed childhood sweetheart in Private Ceremony!*

Art and Marion were engaged and planning a wedding for the next year. Things in the Phillifant household had changed too with Muriel now working as a secretary at B.C. Telephone Company's downtown offices, and brother Leslie, or Les as he preferred to be called, working for an advertising agency headquartered in the Marine Building.

Things were a lot easier financially for Alice these days with everyone in the home employed. Will was working at Restmore's and her brother Jack kept busy as a painter/plasterer. Marion was still at Spencer's. Alice could busy herself with what she liked best, running the household efficiently, going to her church group meetings, inviting friends for afternoon tea, or going to one of their home's for the same. And in the evenings she would sew or embroider, do some tatting, crocheting or knitting. She used to say, "the devil finds work for idle hands."

With Jack sitting in his chair listening to the radio and reading, Will would often retreat to the back lane after supper where the ring of horseshoes could be heard as he and his brother Fred got a game together, sometimes ending in a dust-up over the score. Tweed caps would be flung to the ground, and sparks would fly. Art sometimes refereed as he waited for Marion and Muriel to do the dinner dishes. The latter was a bone of contention with Marion who felt it unfair, that although she'd worked all day and had a date waiting, she still had to do dishes first, while Muriel usually had no date or plans for the evening. At one point she became so exasperated with her sister who kept making her re-wash a plate, she picked it up and broke it over her head! She thought it hilarious, Muriel thought otherwise. Through the years they often talked about that little sequence. I don't know if either ever forgave the other.

Now that she and Art were betrothed, Marion was going to have to pass the Cupit/Davies test. She was invited to a family dinner with all in attendance. To her consternation, Uncle Tom Davies, insisted she sing a solo for them. Whispering Hope was her choice, a duet she and Lillian had often sung at church. She passed the test, afterwards telling Art she'd almost sung "I Don't Want To Play In Your Yard, I Don't Like You Anymore." It was a silly song from her repertoire, one she often sang along with Waltz Me Around Again Willy and Roll Out the Barrel. Uncle Tom would not have thought such songs appropriate for a young lady. She did have a lovely soprano voice and often sang solos. At the other extreme, and to Art's consternation, she could also yodel.

The wedding of the year, *(in the eyes of the Cupit family and McLarnin fans)* was about to take place. The minister from Grandview United would officiate at the ceremony and Lillian had asked Marion to decorate their home for the event. All the furniture was moved out of Grace and Harry's living room for the big day and in front of the new lace panels on the one front window an arch covered with fresh fragrant white lillies was set up. A large wedding bell covered in white satin petals and fresh pink rosebuds hung from the centre of the arch. As the few close relatives took their places on chairs set up in the dining room, policemen stood at the front and back doors of the house checking everyone's identity before letting them inside while trying to keep the crowds who had gathered outside away from the house, for the wedding's location had leaked out and newspaper photographers were in the crowd.

Following the ceremony, the bride and groom were to be whisked away by car to an undisclosed spot from where they would later leave by ship for a honeymoon in Honolulu. With crowds lining the streets outside the Cupit home, the decision was made to hide the car in the basement garage and get the newlyweds to lie low on the floor of the back seat covered with blankets as Art *(their designated getaway driver)* left, seemingly alone in the vehicle. And that's how their escape was made and the press momentarily foiled.

By the time the last of the autumn leaves had been raked and burnt and Vancouverites began to turn their thoughts to another cold Depression winter, Lil and Jimmy were residing in New York City. Although living a glittering life in a fabulous Fifth Avenue apartment as Jimmy trained for an upcoming match, Lil was hoping to return to her parent's for Christmas that year, and to see her baby nephew, Bob, born to Frank and Marg that November. Grace and Harry now had two grandchildren and a purebred Chinese chow pup to occupy their time. Shiu *(shoe)* had been given to Jimmy as a gift from an admirer, but he and Lillian were unable to take the dog to the U.S. with them. And so Shiu became Harry's and Grace's beloved companion. Their daughter may have been far away in New York, but Shiu followed Grace everywhere as she did her chores, never getting far from her side until early evening when Harry came home from work. Then Shiu was there at the back gate, tail wagging, to welcome him. He would always pretend the black-tongued purebred was a nuisance, but everyone knew better.

Nineteen thirty-six dawned and the new city hall looking for all the world like an ornate wedding cake, sitting atop the hill at Cambie and 12th Avenue was finally nearing completion and would be unveiled at the start of festivities to honor the 50th anniversary of Vancouver's incorporation as a city. Golden Jubilee festivities were being planned perhaps with the intent to rival the three hour extravaganza "The Great Ziegfeld" opening in movie theatres at a preported cost to Metro of $500,000 an hour. Sir Percy Vincent, Lord Mayor of London, had been invited to preside over the jubilee celebration and would present Vancouver's mayor with a grand-looking ceremonial mace.

Out in the 800 block of Granville Street, Oreste Luigi Notte opened a shop called Bon Ton, which would specialize in French and Italian style pastries, cakes and cookies. It would become famous for delectable goodies and it's tea room where Vancouver ladies in hats and gloves met to take high tea. But popular and beautiful as his cakes were, they were also pricey.

Chapter 11

Another Bride, Another Groom

Alice Phillifant was busy in her own kitchen mixing and baking the fruit cake in pans especially crafted by Art for the triple tiered wedding cake for his and Marion's marriage on March third. She was also putting the finishing touches on Marion's wedding gown. Although it was Depression days and money was tight, this first wedding in the Phillifant family was not to be soon forgotten. Sixty-five guests were invited with invitations hand-lettered in Marion's fine script, and as March was not a month when garden flowers abounded, she had been making hundreds of daffodils from crepe paper which she intended to mix with as many fresh picked pussy-willows and greenery as possible. Grandview United Church with its iron tracery balconies was to become a virtual garden for the ceremony. Will was trying to force some spring flowers in his greenhouse to decorate the bridal table for the home reception. He didn't own a car, and neither did anyone else in their household, so the plan was to get up early on the morning of the wedding, pick whatever was available in the garden, and then he and Marion would walk down to decorate the church.

The morning of March 3rd everyone awoke to a snowfall! Much moaning went on as they tried to pick bits of greenery and half-frozen pussy-willows, placing them in buckets to carry the three blocks to Grandview United. The snow subsided by late afternoon, but it was still going to be a very cold evening. Family members kept muttering about what a stupid idea it was to be getting married at the beginning of March of all times.

But by 7 p.m. as the pipe organ's mellow tones filled the church and candlelight's glow danced on the amber-paned windows, all was right. The Reverend Galloway , groom and groomsmen took their places. The congregation and choir began singing the hymn "O Perfect Love" as Marion in ivory satin, her bridesmaid Muriel in gold and flower-girl, cousin Ruthie in pink, prepared to go up the aisle. But where was Will? At the last minute a late guest had come to the door of the church and found it locked, as was the custom once the bride had arrived. Will had taken it upon himself to go outside and around to the back door of the church to let him in. He then walked through the church, fresh snowflakes dotting his hair and dusting the shoulders of his tuxedo, smiling and nodding to guests as he made his way to the back where Marion was waiting to make her entrance on his arm. I can well imagine Alice's indignation at the series of events.

A reception was held at Will and Alice's home afterwards. And as the festivities carried on, Art and Marion left for a honeymoon trip by the late night sailing to Victoria. The voyage complete with stateroom cost $3.50 as did their stay at the Glenshiel Hotel on the corner of Elliott and Douglas Streets, a block from the Parliament Buildings. A brochure from their hotel mentions such attributes as an open fireplace in the drawing-room and steam-heating throughout with telephones and reading lamps in each room. After following the birds to Victoria, they journeyed by car via the ferry Iroquois to Seattle on the Black Ball Line. For depression times, this was almost a luxury trip.

Returning to Vancouver, the newly married couple lived in a small house in the 2700 block of East 15th. Not working anymore, for at this time if a woman married she could not work, Marion slipped easily into the role of homemaker. Things had picked up a bit at the shop where Art worked, but for many men still unable to find employment the situation was grave. By April, two thousand men, fed up with living in relief camps on 20 cents a day and board, marched angrily into Vancouver. It was a tense situation. The mob took over and occupied the Hudsons Bay Store where they smashed windows and display cases. They also occupied the Library on Main and Hastings where more destruction took place. Mayor Gerry McGeer was forced to read the riot act. Policemen on horseback rounded up people. There were many injuries and much damage before things began to cool down. By June many of these same unemployed would march on Ottawa, gathering support and momentum as they rode the rails from B.C. across Alberta and the prairie provinces.

With the advent of autumn, Grace and Harry decided to sell Art and Marion the piece of property adjoining their place so they could build a proper house. Plans were drawn up by Will who would do most of the construction, but it would be a family-team effort. He had recently helped build a house on Venables next to his own place, for nephew Jack and his wife Millie Phillifant, and would now use similar plans for Marion and Art's bungalow. The foundation, and any brickwork would be done by Harry, Uncle Jack Warne would do all the plastering and painting, and although he would help with everything, Art's main role would be the plumbing and heating. Construction wouldn't begin until the following spring. They would have the winter months to dream about the project. It was an exciting challenge planning an affordable house in the thirties.

In New York City, Jimmy was ready for a return bout in the ring at Madison Square Gardens for the night of November 20th. Lillian had never been to any of his fights, but this time was persuaded to sit ringside for the event. She was not keen on the idea. Tonight's fight which would be his third *(since his marriage 16 months before to Lil)* would be against Tony Canzoneri. Back home in Vancouver, the entire family was glued to their radios, as was most of Vancouver that winter evening. Baby Face McLarnin was going to make them proud again! They didn't know he had promised Lillian this would probably be his last fight.

As Jimmy told it many times later, he was hit in the 2nd round, saw a million stars and didn't wake up 'til the ninth! He took the worst beating in his 13 year pro boxing career that night as Lil watched. He'd found his final foe although he made $60,000 *(tax free)* for the pain. Eight months later in a re-match he would whip Canzoneri and then easily beat champ Lou Ambers of whom he quipped, "the only time he touched me was when we shook hands before the first round." But it was time to quit. His manager told him, "you've got all the money you'll ever need, Jimmy boy and you've still got your faculties." He left the boxing world with a record of 63 wins, 11 losses and 3 ties and entered the B.C. and Canadian Sports Hall of Fame. McLarnin said, "I was in the boxing game for the money. There's no romance in fighting if you're the one getting beaten up." When he hung up his gloves he was a month shy of his 29th birthday. He and Lil would now move to California and make their home on Sunset Plaza Drive in Beverly Hills.

The curtains were closing on the year 1936, when most of the world was shocked to hear Edward VIII announce his abdication in favor of his brother on December 11th. He would now be known as the Duke of Windsor, and George VI and Elizabeth would become England's monarchs.

Construction of the First Avenue viaduct, just a couple of blocks below Harry and Grace's house began in 1937. This east end of False Creek Flats which had been filled in with soil taken years ago from the 50 metre wide Grandview Cut would soon see plenty of action as more industry moved in. Substantial houses, some of brick, which rimmed Clark Drive and had once overlooked the waters of the flats, were now marooned incongruously with nothing to view other than concrete stanchions. As the viaduct went up, so did hobo jungles, using the new structure for shelter. The mayor and cities's police force had their hands full trying to roust the vagrants and move them on. Most of them had arrived in Vancouver from colder parts of the country, hoping to survive winter in gentler climes.

On Graveley Street, construction was going ahead on Art and Marion's new house that May as the news stories from London told all about the coronation of George VI and Elizabeth at Westminster Abbey. Ties to Britain were still very strong and most stores and many homes in Grandview and other parts of Vancouver were decorated with patriotic bunting, flags and pictures of the royal couple.

By fall the finishing touches were put on the two bedroom bungalow at 1416 Graveley. Painted cream and brown, it had a rough textured California stucco on the bottom and cedar shingles on the upper portions. Leaded glass windows made by Will decorated the coved ceilinged living room where he'd also built in a bookcase/china cabinet with glass doors trimmed with some of his fretwork. Harry's contribution, besides the chimney, was a fireplace containing several accent tapestry bricks reportedly left over from work he did on one of the 18 fireplaces in the Rogers mansion. Marion said he had brought one brick home in his lunch pail each night, but Harry just looked amused and puffed on his pipe, whenever this was suggested. A small entry hall, kitchen, dining room, and one bathroom completed the main floor. Two bedrooms were upstairs and a full basement down. By no means ostentatious, it was theirs and like the cottage in Wind In The Willows it was *"a capital little house compact and well-planned! Everything there and everything in its place."* Out back by the lane, the old boxy garage built years before by the Cupit brothers still loomed, and Grace's clothesline remained running from a corner pole to her back porch. They would have to stay put for now, as would what was left of Grace's vegetable garden.

Art and Marion moved in ready to celebrate their first Christmas in their own home. Cards they sent out that year bore a black and white picture of the two of them smiling contentedly, sitting in their new living room. It would be the last Christmas they'd sit quietly by the fireside pondering the future. Things were about to change.

Emma Jane Bird Warne and John Josiah Warne, Plymouth, England, April 1872

Alfred, Emma, Alice and Jack with their mother Emma Jane (Bird) Warne

Will Philifant and the Kallaway Brothers outside the tiny house they built at Cedar Cove, circa 1905

Clearing property in early Vancouver. Tom Davies on the right.

Picnic in the woods, Vancouver 1910
From left to right: Jack & Helen Warne, Elsie Phillifant, Fred and Will Phillifant, Alice Warne and baby Jack Phillifant

William and Alice Phillifant on their wedding day, Vancouver B.C., July 29, 1911.

Helen Warne holding Marion, Alice Phillifant and Jack Warne. Prince Albert Street.

Grandpa William Phillifant

The Moore's: Mervyn, Gwynn and their mother Matilda (nee Phillifant)

Grace and Harry Cupit's house at 1606 McLean Drive

Alice and Will Phillifant's house at 2162 Venables St.

Grandview United Church, 1885 Venables St, circa 1956. Presently the Vancouver East Cultural Centre

Mary (Renowden) Davies with husband Tom and child outside the shop, 1941 Commercial Drive

Marion, Les and Muriel in the raspberry patch on Venables Street

Grace Cupit with sons Ernie, Jack, Frank and Arthur before sailing to Canada, 1912

The original Lumberman's Arch in Stanley Park, 1920

Lillian Cupit and Jimmy McLarnin's June wedding. Pop Foster was best man, Margaret Davies, bridesmaid

Arthur and Marion Cupit on their wedding day, Vancouver B.C., March 3, 1936

Joan Cupit, 1943

A Graveley Street Parade, 1945
From left: Carolyn and Donna, Linda, Norm, Ellen, Shirley, Joan, Anita and Jeannie

Marion, Joan, Norm and Art under the willow tree, summer of 1942

The Cupits, 1943
Back: Jack & Marion, Harry & Grace, Ernie & Elsie, Art & Marion, Frank & Marg
Front: Marilyn, Bob, Joan, Norm and Don

Grandpa Harry Cupit and Shiu

Eleanor Agnew Phillifant and Joan

April 1942 - Grandma and her son Les before leaving for war

Air raid practice. Art and sister-in-law Muriel, circa 1942

Joan and the Model A Ford, 1942

Joan, Norman, Ted and Bill on Stanley Park Seawall, 1951

Actress Lillian Carlson riding in the PNE float designed by Marion Cupit for the Totem Theatre production of Born Yesterday.

The Grandview United Church Choir, 1955

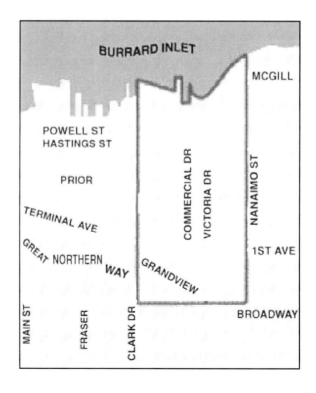

The Highland Echo

ficial organ of the Grandview Chamber of Commerce

1c.

Autumn Opening
1922

Just Chatter

(text illegible)

SHOWS AND STARES

(text illegible)

Eat More Pie

(text illegible)

Keep Your Pants Pressed and Your Shoes Shined.

WE WONDER WOULD IT WORK? *(text illegible)*
"DEPOSIT RUBBISH ON THE SIDEWALKS."

Services at Local Churches

St. Saviour's Anglican

(address line)
REV. SAMUEL PEA M.A., Ph.D., Rector
11 A.M.—MATINS AND HOLY COMMUNION
2:30 P.M.—SUNDAY SCHOOL
4:30 P.M.—HOLY BAPTISM
7 P.M.—EVENSONG

(text illegible)

Robertson Presbyterian

(address line)
REV. ALEX EILER, D.D., Pastor
11 A.M.—Devotional Building
7:30 P.M.—Fact, First and Last

Grandview Baptist

(address line)
Pastor
REV. WALTER DANIEL, B.A.
R. CHAS. HUGHES, Chorister
11 A.M.—COMMUNION SERVICE
12:15 A.M.—BIBLE SCHOOL
7:30 P.M.—"Can We Have Definite Knowledge of Our Acceptance With God?"

Grandview Methodist

Corner Victoria Drive and Venables Street
PASTOR: REV. R. K. MIDDLETON
CHOIR LEADER: MRS. J. V. BETTS
11 A.M.—Testimony.
Children Talk "Lourens"
ANTHEMS
"Behold a King Shall Reign" Foster
"Set Your Affection on Things Above" Scott
2:30 P.M.—SUNDAY SCHOOL and BIBLE CLASS
3:30 P.M.—A String of Pearls
An Address for Young People on Character Building
ANTHEMS
(text illegible)
EVERYBODY WELCOME TO OUR SERVICE

Trinity Methodist Church

(address line)
Pastor Rev. J. D. HIGGINS
Choir Leader: MR. M. A. NEVILLE
11 A.M.—Rev. J. D. Hansen.
ANTHEMS
"The Earth Is The Lord's" Danks
Solos: *(illegible)*
2:30 P.M. SUNDAY SCHOOL
7:30 P.M. Rev. J. D. Roberts.
Soloist: Mr. J. D. Clarke.
ANTHEM
(text illegible)

TRADE OR EXCHANGE

(text illegible)

FOR SALE

(text illegible)

Society

(text illegible)

FOR RENT

(text illegible)

(text illegible)

Grandview Florist

(text illegible)

McComber Bros.
BUTTER, EGGS & CHEESE

(text illegible)

Local Stores Give Better Values
Echo Ads. Will Save You Money

Part 2

Growing Up In Grandview

Chapter 12

No Mere Visit

When humorist Stephen Leacock visited Vancouver he said, "if I had known what it was like, I wouldn't have been content with a mere visit. I'd have been born here." And I was; brought home from Grace Hospital that autumn day in 1938 to the capital little house my Dad and two grandfathers had built for us on Graveley Street. It was right next door to my Grandma and Grandpa Cupit who, instead of being on hand to greet me, had the audacity to leave town, travelling by ship to England to visit relatives. One could hardly blame them however, for talk of war was much in the air. Upon their return they gifted me with a genuine Winnie the Pooh bear and all was forgiven.

As it goes with most first babies, I was dressed up and displayed at every opportunity. My Uncle Les took 16 millimeter films and roll upon roll of pictures of me, culminating in a show of black and white portraits at The Vancouver Art Gallery where we won awards!

But I wasn't the only production that year. Snow White hit the screens of movie theatres across the country and in November as the populace and their brollys splashed their way through unforgiving rains, the graceful spans of the new Lions Gate Bridge linked Vancouver and the Stanley Park causeway to the North Shore. As the Guiness family had figured, expansion on the north shore including the British Properties was phenomenal. The two-lane bridge was already too small for the traffic, perhaps encouraging some citizens to take up another habit to be blamed on the Guinesses.

Unemployment was still a dark specter and while newspapers in Ottawa were saying the Depression was over, there were more transients hanging about in Vancouver than ever before. Then 1,600 unemployed men stormed and occupied the Art Gallery and the Post Office. Extensive damage was done to both during the 30 days they held forth in the two structures. When the RCMP and local police used tear gas to evict the intruders, vicious riots broke out on the cities streets. Before it was over 40 people had been injured and 21 arrested. Property damage mounted to $39,000. This would be the last great riot of the Depression.

Canada's Prime Minister Mackenzie King headed a delegation that visited Germany, and upon returning home said he'd met Hitler and found "great compassion" in the man's eyes! Poor old Mackenzie King should have stayed home and consulted his dog on that one.

Finishing touches were put on the Georgia Viaduct and the new Hotel Vancouver, which opened in May 1939 on its present Georgia Street location. The new copper domed edifice between Burrard and Hornby Streets was completed just in time for a royal visit from King George VI and Queen Elizabeth who probably never noticed the spiffy new roof. As they sped by 1st Avenue in their royal maroon McLaughlin Buick, crowds of union jack waving Grandviewites including Mom, Dad and eight month old me, lined the streets. Uncle Les had brought a portable observation tower *(a.k.a. stepladder)* where he perched high above us to better photograph the monarch. I probably was not the only one who viewed the whole thing as a blur, for they drove past at crack speed, probably because the newly crowned monarch was suffering from a bout of food poisoning.

Grandpa Phillifant, my maternal grandfather busied himself that spring of '39 landscaping our Graveley Street property. He planted a weeping willow tree which in later years would block up the drains, a mock orange that gave Dad hay-fever, English holly and boxwood that would always need clipping, and lace cap hydrangeas so hardy they eventually became the front garden's feature. Things seemed calm enough. The little house was looking good, its front window box brimming with fragrant yellow, orange and red wallflowers. New lawns had weathered the drumming rains of the past winter, and on the boulevard Grandma Cupit's golden-chain *(laburnum)* trees, interspersed with the city's mountain ash were poised, ready to mess up the sidewalks again with their falling berries and pods.

My Uncle Jack, Aunt Marion and 3 year old cousin Marilyn also had a new house, a large pink stucco bungalow on the corner of West 23rd and Yukon not far from the city hall. Now working at the main B.C. Electric building, Uncle Jack's days of duty in the "sticks" of Ruskin were behind him.

Uncle Frank, now teaching in a city school, had with Aunty Marg and their two sons *(my cousins Bob and Don)* settled into their own home too on the birch tree lined corner of West 35th and Wallace where all their growing up years would be spent.

In June, Grandma and Grandpa Cupit flew to Los Angeles to stay with Aunty Lillian and Uncle Jimmy for the birth of their first child... Ellen, my first American cousin. Grandma reportedly didn't have a lot to do in the nursery department, for baby Ellen had a nursemaid to care for her every wish. This baffled Grandma who returned to Vancouver saying she'd never heard of such nonsense. Imagine one child having to have a nursemaid! She'd crossed the Atlantic with four active little sons and then traveled across Canada by train with them. No nursemaid had helped her!

The Wizard of Oz premiered that year and Somewhere Over the Rainbow was being sung by everyone who'd fallen in love with a pigtailed, red haired Judy Garland. In Europe, Adolph Hitler was following his own yellow brick road as he swept through and annexed Czechoslovakia. And then in the early morning hours of September 1, the German armies marched into Poland. On September 3, the British and French declared war on Germany.

Sandwiched in between these earth-changing days, September 2nd was my first birthday, celebrated in the usual fashion with one-candled cake, all grandparents present, and many presents. Uncle Les was there too, camera in hand to record the event in pictures he would later hand-tint. What thoughts were in the family's heads that evening with hourly news bulletins crowding the airwaves? Certainly they must have wondered what the future held.

Writer Torchy Anderson wrote the following, date-lined September 9th, "By official proclamation Canada moved into the world war at midnight. But it was during a casual, undramatic moment when the Commons clock pointed to 10:23 p.m. *(eastern daylight time)* that the country actually made its decision to enter its second great war beside Britain and France. Part of the reason it took Canada longer to join the war was that the parliament had to be recalled for a special emergency session. Some members traveled by plane but most traveled from all parts of Canada on trains, which took days."

Chapter 13

The War Years Begin

And so the years of war began, with Canada's three services totaling about 10,000 men plus their militia known as "Saturday Night Soldiers," trained only in the basics and with poor equipment. According to Barry Broadfoot's book, Six War Years, "The army in 1939 could have mustered something like 29 Bren machine guns, 23 antitank rifles and 5 three-inch mortars." Not too daunting to the enemy. Our country's Navy was not in much better shape with six decrepit destroyers, while our Air Force existed in name only, reataining 4,000 men. Canada had no defense budget and no war industry.

On the surface life didn't change noticeably for most Vancouverites that year or the early part of 1940. The war still seemed remote; something one read about in the Daily Province or Vancouver Sun. It was all happening "over there." That June my Uncle Ernie married Elsie Squires whose parents owned the Magnet Hardware on Commercial Drive where she and her sister Verna worked. I was too young to go to the wedding which took place at Grandview United with my Daddy and three uncles in the wedding party, but many years later at their house on the corner of East 5th and Garden Drive, Aunty Elsie would let me take the satin gown from her cedar chest and try it on for dress-up.

Theatre Under the Stars *(TUTS)* opened its first season in Stanley Parks Malkin Bowl with a production of The Belle of New York. Uncle Les's picture appeared in the write-up. He had emerged as a young man with a good tenor voice and promising career. As I was just a toddler, I missed his debut, but other family members went to various performances and said he was wonderful. While artists sang out their hearts to happy audiences beneath the stars, in sharp contrast, the Battle of Britain had begun with the first large-scale bombing raid by Germany on docks in South Wales. By August as the TUTS season closed, the second phase of the Battle had begun with bombing raids on RAF command centers at North Weald and Hornchurch followed by the first RAF raid on Berlin.

National registration was put into effect requiring every person over sixteen years of age to carry a card, on penalty of fine or imprisonment or both. Being a youngster I was luckily exempt. The only other exceptions were cloistered nuns, members of the armed services on active duty, and persons confined to mental institutions. Not much in the way of choices if you toyed with the idea of becoming a dissident. Fascist and communist groups were banned under the War Measures Act and Mackenzie King's Liberals retained the majority in Dominion elections.

The average Canadian income at just $975 that year probably didn't leave much over for home improvement projects, but in case painting was on your agenda a guy in Toronto named Norman Breaky had just invented the paint roller. Although she wouldn't get to use one for a few years, home decorators like Mom, who didn't like to waste time, thought this tool amazing. No more brushes! Great Uncle Jack Warne, still in the plastering and painting business, scoffed at the idea calling it a lot of blinkin' nonsense.

Canada's economy began to boom. Munitions factories were springing up and transport vehicles and tanks now rolled off our assembly lines often manned by very young or elderly workers doing their bit to help the war effort. Grandpa Phillifant, now 62 years of age went to work at the Boeing Plant on 1st Avenue between Main Street and Clark Drive. Wearing his tweed cap, jacket, and pants with bicycle clips, he'd peddle to work, lunch pail strapped on the back of the bicycle seat. At the end of his shift, he'd head up the hill again, sometimes stopping in at our house for a breather and to see what new things I'd been up to. Mom would give him tea and a cookie while I gave him hugs. This being the days before 10 speeds, he probably needed a rest prior to tackling the rest of the hills up towards Commercial Drive. After that he'd have an easier ride on flatter ground as he headed home along Victoria Drive to his and Grandma's house in the 21st hundred block of Venables Street.

In the spring of 1941 North Vancouver's Ferry # 5 was launched at Coal Harbour to shuttle passengers and cars back and forth across to the foot of Lonsdale. My brother Norm was born that June. It was a difficult birth however, he was a tiny baby that would need to undergo several surgeries, a daunting thought to Mom and Dad in those premedical insurance years.

As rationing began spreading, stores like the Piggly Wiggly at the top of Graveley and Commercial where Mom and Grandma shopped would place signs in their windows saying Sugar ½ lb wk per person, Tea ½ of usual purchase, coffee ¾ of usual purchase and so on. McCombers in the 1600 block of the Drive was where we purchased our eggs, cheese and butter. There was sawdust on the floors behind the counter, and cheese was selected from huge rounds. Eggs were placed in brown paper bags, which we'd carry home very carefully. None of the rationing in effect worried me much until it came to the butter. Mom would take the pound of butter and section it off, placing tiny toothpick flags with our names on our allotted amount for the week. Then as now, I loved my bread and butter. Luckily since my new brother was not into it yet, I got to enjoy his share. Mom and my two grandmother's were busy like other Grandview housewives finding ways to produce eggless, fatless, sugar limited cakes and cookies. Wacky Cake, a chocolaty invention proved to be a winner. School kids from the neighborhood collected fat and tin foil which they handed in at the weeks end to their teacher to help the war effort.

Oil and gas were rationed so we no longer took a Sunday drive around Stanley Park in our 1929 Ford. Instead, Dad and Mom spent the weekends working on our backyard victory garden. Flowers were replaced with things we could eat and everyone was canning. Once in awhile there'd be an explosion in the basement as a glass sealer of apricots or peaches blew up.

By autumn my favorite Uncle, Les, had joined the army and would all too soon be heading by troop train for training in Dundurn, Saskatchewan. Other servicemen from our West Coast would be sent to Vernon, Sarcee, or Shiloh. From the old gang at Grandview United, our church, 47 had now joined up. One of them was Auntie Muriel's boyfriend whom we affectionately called Tyke. He had dreamed of becoming a commercial pilot and was training with the RCAF. Lots of photos were taken in backyards like ours the Sunday before Uncle Les left. The family all lined up to have one last family portrait. Les's girlfriend Eleanor was there too as he balanced baby Norman on one knee and held a protective arm around me, just recovering from whooping cough. Brave fixed smiles appear on the faces of family members in those pictures. And then the awful day arrived and we all stood on the platform at the train station on Main Street waving our good-byes to dear Uncle Les, all too soon lost in the rush of boarding recruits. Wanting one more glimpse of him, albeit fleeting, and none too clear from a train's window, our family rushed by car up to the Grandview Cut at the end of Commercial Drive and Broadway to look down from the overpass and wave again as the steam train whistled and wended it's way through the tunnel heading out towards the Valley and beyond. And just like that, all had changed. Letters would now be the remaining link to loved ones.

Down in the sunshine of southern California, Uncle Jimmy McLarnin was training troops at Catalina Island and investing money in a war plant when he wasn't appearing at Bond Drives with movie stars. He and Aunty Lillian had welcomed another daughter Jean, born just after Christmas, a sister for Ellen and another cousin for me.

Dad had become a member of the ARP *(Air Raid Protection)* and Auntie Muriel had joined the Red Cross. On weekends they'd practice and drill in Grandma and Grandpa Phillifant's back yard. A metal bucket for sand, another for water, a stirrup pump and gas masks were part of Dad's equipment. The idea being, when an air raid alarm sounded, he would put on his metal helmet and with supplies in hand, walk his designated territory checking to see if people had put their lights out. At least that's the way he explained it all to me. He didn't tell me that if a bomb hit he would hopefully have enough sand to put out an incendiary fire, while his bucket and stirrup pump would be used to spray water. In retrospect, it would have been an impossibility. But to me it all seemed like fun as I watched from the sidelines with my little brother, waiting our turns to try on the gas masks. Grandpa stood by silently, smoking his pipe and likely recalling the full horror of war as he'd experienced it as a Canadian soldier at The Somme.

The seriousness of the situation became apparent when a Japanese submarine was sighted off our coast by fishermen who in true laid-back Canadian fashion didn't bother to turn in their report until after they'd finished their fishing! When an enemy sub actually shelled Estevan Point Lighthouse, we were no longer laughing. One in every 11 Canadians was now in uniform. All persons of Japanese origin on the West Coast were being relocated to interior camps. Soon the well kept truck farms, their neat rows of green produce over looking the winding Fraser River, where we'd often taken a Sunday drive, would fall into ruin and many of the once tidy dwellings would be vandalized.

From April through August, Uncle Les sent me charming illustrated letters, the first of many to follow, telling me all about his first gopher sitings, and about marching, and sleeping in bunk beds and having to line up for all his meals, making it sound like being away at summer camp. In fact he often mentioned Crescent Beach.

Chapter 14

Summer At Crescent Beach

Throughout the war years, most civilians on the home front didn't have time or money for extensive summer holidays. A few days or even a weekend at a place like Cultus Lake, White Rock or our favorite, Crescent Beach, was something to be savored.

The latter part of August was always when Dad took his holiday time. Davies Plumbing and Sheet Metal, the family business at 1943 Commercial owned by his Uncle Tom was quietest then. People hadn't begun to think about new furnaces or hot water tank replacements. Auntie Mary, Grandma Cupit's sister, had owned the summer home at Crescent since the 1920's and graciously let us enjoy it too each summer. As I recall, August always seemed hotter and longer in those bygone years.

Closing up our house in Grandview, we'd pack the model A Ford with enough supplies to outfit an expedition. Some holiday for Mom. She would have to work harder at the old camp than if she'd stayed home with at least a few modern conveniences. In those pre-freeway days the trip to Crescent seemed intolerably long for eager youngsters like Norm and me carrying buckets and shovels in hand the whole way in anticipation of sandy beaches.

And there it was... Auntie Mary's big old red cedar shingled camp straddling a corner piece of syringa-bounded property about a half block from the ocean whose salt laden breezes we could already smell. There was a large roofed-in porch along one whole side of the structure with a big handmade stone fireplace for warming oneself after a summer's eve swim. Fired mostly by snags of driftwood, their phosphorescent colors would spark and dance. We could enjoy the fire or sit outside bathed in the silver of an August moon while listening to crickets and frogs serenading one another in the deep, wide ditches that surrounded the place.

Being a kid, I loved to daydream on the wooden swing which Dad suspended in the kitchen doorway for the duration of our stay, while listening to the comforting sounds of rattling dishes, running water and Mom singing. She always seemed to sing while she swept and cleaned; songs like "My Buddy" or "The White Cliffs of Dover."

Across the road was Camp Alexandra where orphaned youngsters were sent for some summer fun. At least that's what I was told if ever I questioned what they were doing across the road when I'd hear them singing songs or spied on them playing on a roundabout thing that looked like lots of fun. But mostly, they seemed to have to line up for everything, even to walk to the beach. What, I wondered, were orphans and why did they get sent to a camp? Was Annie from the newspaper comics over there? She was the only orphan I knew anything about. I wondered if any of the kids had a dog like Sandy and if the girls had to wear the same red dress every day of their lives?

Choosing the room I'd sleep in for the duration of our holiday time was always fun. There were typical little bedrooms under the rafters with chenille spreads and faded floral wallpaper, but the screened-in front porch room off the living room was my favorite. One could lie back on the real feather bed beneath the comforting wood framed bible quote done in sea shells saying GOD IS LOVE and listen to all the night sounds while breathing in those salty breezes, all the time dreaming about what wonders tomorrow might hold. Failing that, I could always eavesdrop on the adult's conversation in the next room.

Breakfast at Crescent was away more enjoyable than eating back in the city. We'd gather in the old camp kitchen with its skirted kitchen sink, open shelves lined with colorful scallop-edged shelf paper and the prettiest array of sapphire blue glass dishes, the color author John Ruskin once said was appointed by the Deity to be a source of delight. To my way of thinking, everything tasted better served on those blue glass dishes. Even corn flakes. For being summer, we didn't have to contend with oatmeal or cream of wheat. We were on holiday!

The warmth of the freshly kindled stove would remove any dampness from the early morning air and if we were short of milk, my little brother and I would gladly volunteer to run down to the country store for a fresh quart. Skipping along the pebble and shell strewn lanes past little vine-covered cottages heavy with honeysuckle and tumbling wild roses, we'd jingle the coins in the bottom of the glass milk bottle until we arrived at the General Store run by Mr. Gardiner. Then with real cream topped milk in hand we'd wander across the street to peek into the tiny ivy covered post office and telephone exchange which stood very near the railway station. Many holidayers to Crescent Beach passed through that station as few owned cars.

Back we'd go to the camp with thoughts of a boat ride with Daddy under the old train trestle where we'd sometimes sit until a train passed over, then returning to the camp to say with excitement, "Mommy, we just got run over by a train!" She always acted surprised and always gave the same reply, "Oh, you poor little children, are you alright?" Or, maybe we'd anticipate a day spent on the beach, gathering pebbles, poking into tidal pools or building sand castles with moats, all intertwined with running in and out of the water with Dad. Life was good.

When evening came on the backs of pink and orange-fired sunsets and we'd had our fill of the beach, supper would be served outside on the porch. By now the kids over at Camp Alexandra had had their roll call and been put to bed, but we felt lucky knowing now we'd get to walk with the adults along the shell strewn beachfront with it's pretty houses and wild sweet pea bordered pathways until we came to the big white house with the striped green canvas awnings and flagpole. I'd peer over the walls and think how lovely the gardens looked and wonder what kind of people lived in a place so huge. Grandpa Cupit said they were bootleggers and something about ill-gotten gain, but there were many times I thought of pursuing a career in it, just so I could have a place with my very own flagpole.

As we headed back along the water's edge, home to the camp where the fireplace would be stoked and Dad would crank up the big old gramophone in its ornate cabinet, we were content. While the strains of Roses of Picardy sung by a tenor with a very wavy voice serenaded us, we'd sip hot cocoa and then off to bed for another night of dreams every bit as sweet as the sound of the ocean waves crashing in and out.

And then holiday time was at an end. We were back home on Graveley Street where the radio would again be on reporting the War, with which everyone was preoccupied. Why couldn't life forever be the way it was for those two weeks at Crescent?

Chapter 15

Air Raids And Blackouts

On December 9, a story in the Vancouver Sun advised the city's citizens thus: City lights will not be turned on this afternoon except for intersection lights, which the city engineer's department is attempting to make invisible from the air by bluing.

It seemed all I heard about anymore was "the war." By Christmas time the nine o'clock gun that we'd sometimes gone to the Park specifically to hear, as it blasted towards HMCS Discovery, had now been muzzled and the electrified marble Japanese lantern that had once welcomed ships into our beautiful harbor had been turned off. At Ferguson Point, a camouflaged lookout disguised to resemble forest, stood ready, a project Uncle Les had worked on prior to his enlistment. Jericho Beach, now an air force base, was off limits to the public. Barbed wire surrounded it and armed sentry guards patrolled 24 hours a day. Children that had played so care freely on these sand swept beaches, now mimicked the men training within the yards by marching up and down, sticks over their shoulders feigning rifles. War had come to Vancouver.

When air raid sirens wailed, our windows had to be quickly covered with blackout screens and all our lights switched off. With the scream of the sirens Dad and others in the ARP immediately collected their gear and set out to check their assigned parts of the neighborhood house by house for signs of lights. Mom and I would kiss him goodbye as he headed out; hoping it wouldn't be long 'til the all-clear siren sounded so he could return. Sometimes Grandma and Grandpa from next door came over to our house so we could all be together.

Semi blackouts were put into effect now, along with banned porch lights, lighted store windows and all billboard lighting. Car headlights had to be blinded except for a vertical slit three inches long by one-quarter inch wide and taillights could only have small discs in the center. At night, darkened street cars and trams clattered along Commercial Drive, sometimes to be guided in snow or fog by the conductor walking ahead with a flashlight to illuminate the track for the driver.

Hotel Vancouver became a military headquarters around this time and Ottawa ordered chlorination of Vancouver's water supply to protect troops in the area.

Like many other mothers with sons in the service, Grandma Phillifant was knitting for the Red Cross. Her needles would click click away as she produced v-neck sleeveless sweaters, sox with double heels and flat toes, two way mitts and body belts, all done in khaki or heather color wool for the army. She sewed too, surgeon's caps and gowns and hospital gowns.

Grandpa Phillifant spent hours in his retreat, the basement workshop, where on weekends and evenings he busied himself making presents for Christmas. A doll house for me and train engine for Norman to ride upon were the main gifts, but he also created a board game for the family. He called it Convoy and unveiled it for the first time following Christmas dinner and carol singing 'round the piano. Although I was too young to play the game, many happy hours were spent by the adults sitting around Grandma and

Grandpa's oval dining room table beneath the brass and opal glass chandelier, nibbling Welch's chocolates while pondering their next move. The game consisted of tiny battle ships on a board representing the Atlantic Ocean. The object being to get one's ships and cargo through enemy lines unscathed. Many years later a game called Battleship *(all plastic)*, but highly reminiscent of Grandpa's hand-crafted game, hit the markets. He never thought of patents when he came up with a new invention. Too bad because early the next year he was hard at work building a table top hockey game with paddles on either side, the prototype of Foozball. Again, no patent!

December of 1941 had seen the U.S.A., Britain and Canada declare war on the Japanese, following the attack on Pearl Harbor, a day President Roosevelt said would go down in infamy. Malaya, Manila, Hong Kong, Guam, Midway and Wake Island were next to be raided by the Japanese and by Christmas time British, Indian and Canadian troops had surrendered Hong Kong to them. Manila and Burma would fall to the enemy next, followed by the Solomon Islands and Borneo. In January the Americans sent their first troops to Britain. Indeed it seemed the entire world was now at war on all fronts.

Tyke, that eager young man from Grandview Young People's had wound up in north western Alaska where the RCAF would play a vital role on that front with the Americans against the Japanese in the Aleutians. The flying weather was consistently grim and treacherous for these men whose duties required them to fly over fogged-in waters and colorless tundra.

He sent souvenirs home for Auntie Muriel; fringed pink and blue satin pillow covers bearing pictures of huskies and Eskimos with spears and polar bears. I was fascinated and wondered why she kept them in her bedside table along with letters telling of the adventures he was having in the land of the midnight sun. When a lengthy story and his picture appeared in the Daily Province that November telling all about Vancouver's contribution to the war in

the north, she kept that too. By now, 28 years old and working as a
secretary at B.C. Telephone, she told Mom she just longed to get
out of Vancouver and do something more fulfilling than weekend
Red Cross work.

And then she heard of a way she could share in victory building
in the hectic, teeming city of wartime Washington D.C., for with
the entry of the States into the war, Washington had become
headquarters for the allied nations for the pooling of huge stores of
war materials. Eleven United Kingdom missions and six combined
supply and military boards were headquartered in the capital city
and workers were desperately needed. Secretarial and clerical posts
were available in many of the British offices there. The idea of helping
to win the war from an office desk in the "world's capital" appealed
to Auntie Muriel and she sent off her application to work for the
British Embassy.

Now came the news that Tyke, lost during a flying mission in
the North while preparing for the onslaught on Kiska, first listed as
missing in action, was presumed dead. The terrible announcement
was made at church that Sunday and a star placed next to his name
on the board in the narthex listing all those from our congregation
in service for King and Country.

> *But War's a Game,*
> *Which Were Their Subject's Wise,*
> *King's Would Not Play At.*
> William Cowper, from The Winter Morning Walk.

Chapter 16

From Grandview To D.C.

Aunty Muriel was getting settled in her new job with the British Embassy where she'd been hired at $150 per month plus 10% adjustment, $31.50 subsistence allowance and full first class railway fare provided. In her own words, following tearful farewells to all of us in Vancouver, she described the train trip that took five days.

"My first glimpse of the Rockies. There's snow on the high peaks and it's mid-August! Arriving in Calgary 3 hours late, after a breakdown east of Banff, I made a mad scramble for the train at St. Paul where I was rewarded by the thrilling Hiawatha streamliner trip to Chicago. The vastness of Chicago's station awed me as did the dirt and heat of the Chicago-Washington train. Finally, the exciting evening arrival in a melting Washington after having stood all the way from Baltimore, fearful I'd miss my stop"!

For several months Muriel lived at the Meridian Hill Hotel on 16th Street, touted as Washington's new and exclusive hotel for women. Strict rules for residents applied. There was to be no cooking or cooking utensils of any kind in the rooms, no radios played before 9:00 a.m. or after 11:00 p.m., and no gentlemen callers allowed above the 1st floor at anytime!

The Meridian had a dining room where meals could be taken, but no girl wearing slacks would be admitted. Writing to Mom, she said her first big "home was never like this" impression came with the realization that three times a day, month in, month out, she'd have to eat restaurant food. Whether it was southern fried chicken at Evans Coffee Shop in Arlington, (5 minutes from the White House) or the 35 cent special at Sholl's Colonial Cafeteria on Connecticut Avenue which advertised, "Many food items still at Depression Prices! Eat at Scholl's and you can buy more war bonds", it was still eating out and she missed Grandma's home cooking.

In working for the British Ministry of Supply, Auntie Muriel was with the oldest and largest British Mission in the U.S., responsible for the procurement of all war office equipment, machine tools and much miscellaneous equipment on behalf of other government departments in the U.K. The ministry was linked closely to the British Army Staff. At this time, each British Dominion: Canada, Australia, New Zealand, South Africa, Southern Rhodesia and India maintained it's own purchasing or procurement mission in the U.S. with headquarters in Washington.

The staff filling secretarial and clerical positions often worked long hours. Because wartime Washington had a shortage of office space many offices were set up in hallways, libraries, kitchens and bedrooms of fine old homes. For a time Aunty Muriel worked out of a tiled bathroom tucked away in a corner of the impressive Andrew Mellon mansion. He had been U.S. ambassador to Britain until 1933 and left his extensive art collection and a gallery building to the American people upon his death in 1937. She wrote home telling us how the head of another Mission directed his staff from the fascinating Chinese Room in the home of a Washington Senator while a typing pool of Vancouver girls operated from the drawing room of another historic home. Other employees daily tread the beautiful marble staircase of a former Dupont residence as they reported for duty each morning. Her glimpses of wartime

Washington often found their way into Grandview's local paper, The Highland Echo.

Life in the District of Columbia was a far cry from Muriel's former existence. She wrote telling us about sight-seeing trips and concerts given by the likes of Claudio Arrau. She attended many plays at the National Theatre with Broadway casts from New York. At Constitution Hall she heard the Philadelphia Orchestra with Eugene Ormandy conducting and the debut performance of the Watergate Symphony on the Potamac under Dr. Hans Kindler's baton. On a trip to New York in March, 1943 she saw the first performance at the St. James Theatre of Rogers and Hammerstein's Oklahoma with Alfred Drake and Joan Roberts in the lead.

As Mom peeled potatoes freshly dug from our Victory garden and prepared the evening's meal from rationed food, while baby Norman fussed in his high chair and I demanded her attention, there must have been times she envied her sister's new life. When she received a program listing names like Paul Whiteman conducting the Army Air Force Band in a rendition of Gershwin's Rhapsody in Blue, or mentions of the day Aunty Muriel met the Duke of Windsor outside the Canadian Legion Hall, or her encounter and chat with Eleanor Roosevelt as they walked along Connecticut Avenue, life on Graveley Street must have indeed seemed flat.

While strains from the wooden radio on our kitchen counter played Vaughn Monroe crooning, "When the Lights Go On Again All Over the World," Mom hummed along while doing her household chores. Excitement abounded whenever the red Royal Mail truck stopped outside our house. I'd watch from the window as the uniformed postman came running up to our front porch, package in hand and rang our doorbell. Gifts postmarked Washington D.C. from Auntie Muriel or from Holland where Uncle Les now was were especially exciting. A beautiful doll called Mistress Mary and a real colonial styled cardboard playhouse which when assembled was big enough for two kids to play inside were wonderful surprises from the States, as were authentic Dutch caps, wooden shoes, bracelets, postcards and story books from the Netherlands.

Rains pelted and soaked the fallen leaves of autumn, winds sweeping them along the ditches and into the gurgling gutters as skies once so full of sunlight, birdsong and hydrangea blue began to take on a pewter cast. Winter was readying another visit upon Grandview.

Now five years old, I was taking piano lessons from Irene Kallaway Sykes whose father Jimmy Kallaway had been Grandpa Phillifant's buddy from the old days when as young lads fresh from Devon, they had bached together as pioneer house builders at Cedar Cove.

It was Great Aunt Matilda Phillifant Moore's piano that now sat beneath the leaded glass piano window in our living room. The upright was a Henry Herbert and Grandpa Cupit said it was named after him. I was only five, but I knew he was teasing. After all, who would ever name a piano after a mandolin-playing bricklayer? Aunt Til's son Mervyn had learned to play on that very instrument in the years prior to his departure for overseas, and when the piano was delivered to our house a solitary piece of sheet music remained in the hinged wooden bench... The Colonel Bogey March!

Ever since coming from England with her two sons Gwynn and Mervyn, to reside in Vancouver, Aunt Til who was Grandpa Phillifant's sister, had worked as a housekeeper to supplement her war widow's pension. She lived in a small West End apartment. Now with Mervyn or "my Mervie" as she referred to him, overseas and her elder son married with two children, when times like Christmas came along she often joined our family.

Small in stature, she was about five feet tall with dark hair flecked with gray and brown eyes that she sometimes squinted at you. An energetic little lady. always a favorite of Mom's, Aunt Til could be counted on to do or say something positively outrageous after which she'd look around to savor the out fall. She seemed to gain great satisfaction from stirring things up. But on the other hand she was kind-hearted, a good cook who intrigued me because when in the kitchen, she wore two aprons, one the conventional way and the other to cover her rump as she had the habit of wiping her hands there. I guess she was a little eccentric for if she had nothing special to do on a given day, she'd often go to a funeral... anybody's! Afterwards she'd drop by our house to tell Mom the details over a "nice cup of tea".

Born and bred an Anglican, she'd usually attend Christ Church Cathedral where the Dean was *(for many years)* Cecil Swanson. After services she liked to corner him and argue a point or two, just she said, to keep him on his toes. Later, when she lived in our neighborhood she'd sometimes visit Robertson Presbyterian Church on Semlin Drive because she enjoyed the preacher there.

Before and after the war Aunt Til would "go home" to Devon and Cornwall to visit her sisters and brothers. I was fascinated hearing about the pixies of Bodmin Moor and she taught me songs like Ilka Moor bar'tat which we sang over and over, laughing and being silly. But it seems family members were not always enthralled by her visits home. When she'd return to Vancouver the phones would ring and then the letters would fly as her kin tried to patch up any misconceptions spread in her wake. Aunt Til would vow never again to return to England, but within a couple of years all was forgotten and off she'd fly to repeat the whole scenario.

Perhaps her outspokenness disturbed people. I really don't know. She was extremely generous with money, of which she never had great amounts and attended every Remembrance Day at Victory Square "for the dear boys", right up until her death in her eighties.

Another Christmas approached and we found ourselves minus the familiar wooden crate of mandarin oranges whose juiciness had long heralded the season. No longer being shipped out of Japan *(with whom we were at war)* we kids had to confront their absence while Dad dealt with gasoline rationing and Mom learned the sale of whipping cream had now been prohibited. She said our mince tarts would have to go naked. Things were indeed looking bleak as the war overseas heated up. Vancouver's radio stations now had to be shut down from 5:30 p.m. and total blackouts were in effect. Eerie, light-less steetcars plied the Commercial Drive tracks and few people ventured out at night. "For Whom the Bell Tolls" and a slew of war inspired movies were showing in theatres like The Grandview, but people thought it risky to be inside a crowded theatre in the event of an attack.

Instead, families cocooned, staying inside contenting themselves with reading, playing card games or singing around the piano. My uncles on the Cupit side of our family all played musical instruments and whenever it was one of their birthdays the family would gather.

When they came to our house accompanied by their wives, my auntie's Marion, Marg and Elsie, I was allowed to greet everyone, then go to bed. I never stayed in it for long, preferring instead to sit half way up the staircase hidden behind the curtain that hung on the landing to cut the winter draft. In one of my cozy flannelette nighties sewn by Mom, and trimmed with eyelet embroidery to make it prettier, I'd sit with my pillow and Winnie the Pooh bear, tapping my toes and fingers to favorite tunes. Lullaby of Broadway, I'm Just a Vagabond Lover, Kitty from Kansas City, Ramona, and Springtime in the Rockies were some of their standards. And in honor of Mom whose middle name was Louise, they'd play the Maurice Chevalier hit, with Uncle Frank doing the famous Parisian's voice, and tossing in some French phrases. Other times Strauss Waltzes with haunting melodies seemed to fill every nook and cranny of our little house. Uncle Ernie played the piano, Uncles Jack and Frank the violin and Dad the saxophone. Being an amateur group, mistakes were made and the brothers would reprimand one another if someone hit a sour note. All was done amidst gales of hearty laughter. At times like this it was hard to remember a war was going on out there.

Chapter 17

Choosing Education

By September of 1944 as Victory gardens produced their bounty and Mom began her canning for another winter, it was time for me to begin grade one at the elementary school on Woodland Drive. I turned six the day school began, and trudged off wearing my new dress and shoes, carrying a pencil box and other supplies. I didn't stay long. After discovering what it was all about, I left the premises and walked back home to the shock of Mom who was just hanging the wash on the line when I pushed open the back yard gate. For two or three days I repeated the performance, saying I already knew how to print a few words and could read a bit, so who needed anything more? I'd decided not to stay, thankyou. Finally, the school principal sat down with me and explained, students could not walk out and return home whenever they felt like it. Conceding defeat and deciding that maybe Miss Francis, my bewildered teacher, wasn't so bad, I complied.

Because Vancouver was an important Pacific coast city that could at any time become a target for enemy bombers, necessary precautions were adhered to in all of the schools, including mine. Regular drills took place. Buckets of sand stood ready at the front of every classroom and we had to learn to hide beneath our desks and cover our heads with our hands whenever the fire bells rang. Then gas masks were donned.

Friday mornings after the Lord's Prayer, said by everyone and led by the teacher, row by row we pupils filed up to her desk to receive a little brown pill. These were iodine tablets to prevent goiter due to wartime shortages in many civilian diets. Some kids thought they tasted horrid, but I liked them, just as I enjoyed my spoonful of Scotts Emulsion, which my brother called Scotch Emotions, every morning.

Depending upon which route was taken; Woodland Elementary School was a five to six block walk from our house. But to get there I had to walk past the gas tanks, which took up a square block between McLean, and Cotton Drives. I had heard adults talking about the tanks being a perfect target for enemy bombers, so upon reaching that street I always ran fast somehow reasoning in my young mind, I'd be safe if only I could make it past those notorious tanks to 4th Avenue. As late autumn set in, mornings and late afternoons were often heavy with fog as smoke from wood and sawdust fueled fires was trapped in the wet, misty atmosphere. Much of the problem was caused by emissions from beehive burners at the numerous sawmills lining the south shores of False Creek. On days thick with fog, the feared gas tanks seemed to vanish. Enroute to or from school, kids like myself breathed a little easier, and strolled past the invisible cylindrical monsters.

"Meet Me In St. Louis" starring Judy Garland and a young Margaret O'Brien was showing in theatres with songs like "Have Yourself A Merry Little Christmas." I wasn't terribly impressed when I heard that my cousin way down in southern California was attending the same school and in the same class as Margaret O'Brien. No, I was too busy that fall preparing for a piano recital, practicing every day after school for an hour. Mom was sewing a pink taffeta dress for me to wear, and I'd been taught to do a dignified curtsy in the event the audience applauded.

Chapter 18

We Had A Woodpile

At some point every summer our relatives, the McLarnins, would descend upon us from their California home for an annual visit. That summer of 1945 was no exception. Auntie Lillian and Uncle Jimmy and their two daughters Ellen and Jean were staying next door to us at Grandma and Grandpas. Such proximity meant we cousins, including my little brother Norm and I, would spend almost a month of those halcyon days from breakfast time on, playing in our yard.

We had a good-sized back yard, fenced all around to keep any pets and us safe from sporadic back lane traffic. Next to our victory garden, a sturdy wooden swing hung from chains attached to a frame beneath the large weeping willow tree, and under the back steps was my tiny lattice enclosed play house where I often whiled away time playing with my dolls and bossing my brother. On rain soaked days, which tended to happen from time to time, there was always the basement to play in although part of it was taken up with a coal bin. Once the bin had held sawdust, but after receiving a decidedly wet load crawling with tiny crabs which scurried all over the basement seeking hiding places, Dad switched to wood and coal for our heat. July and August were prime months to gather a supply for the winter ahead.

In our neighborhood, the appearance of a wood truck was no bigger deal than having the ice man show up with a burlap sack on his shoulder, and large calipers gripping a glistening block of ice destined for our wooden ice box with its heavy hinged lid. Indeed, both coal and ice were delivered *(not at the same time)* by Morrow's whose slogan was "Call to Morrow for Your Ice Today!"

On one of those warm summer mornings full of bird-song and children's laughter, as we played in the back yard with our American cousins, and a new kid from next door called Nicholas Olyinsky, who spoke little English having just recently arrived from Poland, a truck pulled up at our back fence. The driver got out, moved a hinged section and proceeded to back his truck into position as he opened the tailgate. Mom hollered at us kids to stay out of the way as the wood came thundering down in the allotted place next to Dad's gooseberry bushes. After he'd presented the bill and been paid, driver and empty vehicle pulled away leaving us with a mountain of fresh cut pitch-scented firewood. Wow! Ellen and Jean had never seen a woodpile before. This was a first. Woodpiles were unknown in Beverly Hills.

Talk about simple pleasures. A good portion of that morning was spent with the five of us running up, down and around the woodpile. When the novelty finally wore off, having seen how impressed our cousins were, we took them into the basement, along with young Nicholas to play in our coal bin.

For the uninitiated, the object of the game was to run as fast as you could up the sliding stack of coal and then ride it down in a cloud of dust. It made a wonderful noise like a freight train going through a tunnel. Unlike wood which at worst only gave a kid slivers and pitch stains, coal made you absolutely filthy! I imagine the ring on Grandpa and Grandma's tub next door as the cousins cleaned up, matched the grimy one on our bath tub as Mom scrubbed us down all the while berating me for doing such a terrible thing. But how was I to know my cousins pale pink designer togs and white

101

shoes would never clean up? For some reason the coal bin was pronounced off limits to us from then on, and Mrs. Olyinsky refused to let her little Nicholas play with us anymore. Long after the McLarnin's had returned to California, the coal bin episode returned to haunt us, even at Christmas when, in the toe of our stockings Norm and I discovered Santa had left a piece of coal!

Chapter 19

Best Of Friends

It was nearly time to head back to school for grade two, and back to piano lessons for another term. My friend Anita would now be going to Woodland Elementary with me after having been away for a time in Yale. I was glad to have somebody to call on and walk with, although it was usually she who appeared at our back door at twenty to nine.

Anita, or as her mother called her, "Ah Neeta" would continue to be my best friend in the whole world right through to the end of junior high. She, her big brother, parents and paternal grandparents all lived together in a house on two city lots directly opposite my Grandpa's. They had a couple of goats which they tethered to a post on the city owned boulevard which they used as an extension of their property. Chickens squawked and scratched around the small vineyard and huge garden ringed by the largest and most fragrant bushes of rosemary I have ever seen. They grew many other flavorful herbs which were used in their cooking and for healing.

Italians, they had come from Sicily and only Anita and her brother, born in B.C. spoke English. Her grandfather made his living picking dandelions from the rail tracks of the CPR. Her father, always nattily attired came and went on trips; it was rumored, to Chicago or Los Angeles. Roman Catholics, they attended The Church of the Sacred Heart, Vancouver's second oldest Catholic Church, on Campbell and Keefer. Anita, her mother and grandmother seldom missed mass. The men on the other hand seemed to go infrequently. It was generally up to the women to do the praying and church going.

I was always intrigued by the fact their house had two kitchens. In the unfinished basement with its white washed concrete walls reminiscent of a village home in Italy, the floors were dirt with goat skin mats here and there. An old stove fired by wood kept it warm and cozy and produced the delicious crusty home made bread put together daily by the old grandmother in her all black outfit and ever present head scarf. Little nooks and crannies including an underground wine cellar held all nature of preserves. A sturdy old chipped; painted table surrounded by mismatched chairs was where the family ate their meals. Pictures from Italian calendars and a large crucifix hung on the walls. A sink window looked out towards a trellis-enclosed patio covered in season with fat grapes, or empty vines. More unmatched wooden furniture and clay pots holding flowers and herbs were strewn about. Yet upstairs was another world!

There, a modern spotlessly clean white kitchen with electric stove and fridge prevailed. This was where we gathered for Anita's birthday party each year. The rest of that section of the house had shiny hardwood floors, goatskin rugs, niches bearing flickering votive candles and statues of the Blessed Virgin, fine furniture and Italian tapestries. Sometimes at Christmas we sat in the living room to admire the nativity scene always displayed beneath the branches of their Christmas tree. But generally, we had little to do with that section of the house, unless it was to annoy her older brother who had a room set aside for his radios and electronics equipment.

The top floor containing the bedrooms, again was neat and rather sparse except for more religious pictures and some interesting pieces of provincial furniture.

To my knowledge they seldom used their front entrance. There were always people, laughing happy people, greeting one another in Italian, "buon giorno, buona sera or buona notte", coming or going, but always by the basement or side door.

In summer and autumn the music would play into the night as they danced the tarantella, fired by lots of home made wine. This used to drive my very English grandfather crazy. But after putting up with it for well over forty years, he evidently never once complained to them. He'd stand at his living room window, pipe in hand, shake his head and say to me, "Did you ever see the likes of it my lassie, you'd think they were still in Sicily. Tsk, tsk, tsk." Secretly I think he sometimes envied them, especially following my Grandma's death when on warm summer evenings their laughter continued on into the night long after he'd gone to his lonely four-poster bed with nothing to dream on aside from her portrait. His house must have seemed silent... filled with empty rooms.

A pretty girl, Anita had flashing brown eyes and long naturally curly brown hair in which she usually wore a ribbon. She was smart too; able to do arithmetic easily, while I generally struggled. Now we were both in grade two and our teacher was a mean spirited little old white haired lady called Miss Johnston who was forever rapping students on the knuckles with a wooden ruler if they made an arithmetic error. Anita never got smacked.

She had relatives in the film industry in Los Angeles and I had my connections there too with Auntie Lillian and Uncle Jimmy. Coincidentally our U.S. relatives would often send us similarly styled dresses of frills and ruffles with pearl or satin covered buttons. Anita's Mom would look adoringly at us and say in her soft toned voice, "Oh Ah-neeta, you girls should be sisters!"

It seemed to me, Anita's church was always having raffles. I would accompany her as we sold tickets door to door for The Church of the Sacred Heart, although my own church frowned on anything such as games of chance or lotteries. Certain neighbors like the McQuillans or the widow Mrs. Marcasey who lived in the big corner house at the top of our street with all the magnolia trees, were easy marks because they were members of Anita's church. But my Grandpa was another story. Sometimes I used to wonder about him. He never went to church, yet always went on about the works of the devil and so on if we tried to sell him a ticket. We figured it was worth the lecture because although he wouldn't purchase any tickets he'd give us each fifty cents so we could go and buy ourselves some ice cream at the Crystal Dairy.

Chapter 20

We All Scream For Ice Cream

Pushing open the swinging doors of The Crystal Dairy on the corner of Commercial Drive and 4th Avenue, Anita and I stepped up to the towering marble counter. The floors were tiled, the walls were marble interspersed with mirror, and high above us, turning and whirring were big paddle ceiling fans. The whole place seemed cool and our voices echoed when we spoke. It was as if we were encased inside an icicle.

If we were lucky enough to have saved some of our allowance money we'd order a double-decker ice cream cone. When we placed our money upon the counter it too made a hollow clicking noise. The whole place seemed hushed and hallowed. The girl behind the counter would dig down into one of the frost bound bins with her silvery ice cream scoop and position the perfectly formed portion upon each cone. We could hardly wait to start the licking.

If it was a very hot day and we didn't want to go back outside right away, we'd sit by the window at special one-armed chairs much like the ones in school libraries except the wide part of the arms on these was arborite and provided a place for people sipping a big thick milkshake to rest their frosty glass or metal container. On days when it wasn't terribly busy and customers weren't lined up for their shakes or sundaes, we were allowed to stay awhile licking and savoring every chilly mouthful while viewing the streetscape.

As we sat, we could hear the clinking and clattering of milk bottles and metal cases being loaded and unloaded from out back, for that was where the milkmen picked up and ended their deliveries. Milk, Creamo, Half and Half, Whipping Cream and Chocolate Milk called Topsy all came in glass bottles. Ice Cream finished, sweet taste still lingering on our tongues, we'd head outside and around to the back lane where the stable held the Clydesdale horses that still pulled the rubber tired wagons on some of the Grandview routes. Sometimes when we visited we were allowed to give the horses a treat. How lucky we thought those animals were to be living so close to all that delicious ice cream. I think we figured, like stable cats, they got to lick out all the near empty containers.

Sometimes on sticky, sunshiny days when Mom, my little brother and I had gone to the nearby Armenian delicatessen for salads and cold meat for a summertime supper, we'd stop in at the Crystal Dairy and get an ice cream cone to take to Dad a half block away at the shop where he toiled as a sheet metal worker. We'd wave at cousin George in the front glassed in office and go through to the back where Dad in his overalls would be hard at work cutting and shaping metal for furnace pipes and ducting. Upon seeing us, he'd stop, smile one of his beaming smiles, push his cap back on his head and take his handkerchief from his back pocket to wipe his sweating brow. We'd hand him a rather drippy ice-cream cone; vanilla was his favorite, and he'd take a brief break from his labors. He worked very hard, and when he came home at the end of the day, I'd chatter to him from the wooden stool near the wringer washer as he removed his boots and overalls and cleaned up at the basement laundry tub before coming upstairs. Boraxo and a can of something called Snap sat near the soap dish, as did the bottle of Dettol and Band-Aids. As he cleaned his hands, I winced for they were often cut and sore looking. But he never made anything of it.

Chapter 21

How About Some Beethoven?

Funny, but to this day I cannot listen to "A Little Minuet," by Beethoven without thinking of the words someone put to it called "Far Away," which is just where the melody transports me as I drift back to an afternoon in September of that year in our increasingly multi-cultural neighborhood. Maybe the nationalities were a different mix, being then of predominantly English, Scottish and Irish with a few Italians and Germans thrown in for flavor, but blended we were.

At seven years of age, although not a seasoned performer, I never the less had two recitals under my belt and had learned the art of practicing furiously whenever dishes needed to be dried in Mom's kitchen. I could play Swinging Lanterns, The Happy Farmer, Serenade and Little Minuet. It was my favorite. One day in a burst of artistic energy I played it so loud and so often and with so many variations, my little brother shut the piano lid on my fingers. When Mom, who thought it funny, wrote to Uncle Les who was still overseas in the Army, he sent me a letter with a pen and ink drawing of me playing and Norm with an evil look on his face, ready to close the piano's lid.

On this particular afternoon when Anita came to play she brought a new kid along, a quiet dark haired girl. We decided to try out the new kid's yard and check out her stuff. She lived in a house across the back lane from Anita and I realized her father was the peculiar little old junk man who with horse and cart travelled up and down the back streets calling out, "Any old junk?" Then if you had something you wanted to get rid of you stopped him and he climbed down from his cart, looked your junk over, muttering all the while in a strange language and then you argued some more about the price and if you came to an agreement, he carted it away and sold it to somebody else for twice the amount. At least that's what Grandpa told me, and he ought to know because he once let the junk man take an old boiler away and it ended up cut in half, painted red and filled with petunias in Mrs. Roth's front yard. And she paid six dollars for it, and the junk man only gave Grandpa fifty cents. And what was worse, Mrs. Roth was a Liberal! That really bothered Grandpa.

Entering the back garden of the new girl's home, we were disappointed to find the horse wasn't in evidence, obviously kept elsewhere. And any interesting junk was locked inside an old shed. There really was nothing to play with, so we went inside the house for cookies and there in the living room was the shiniest most beautiful piano I had ever seen, with an odd fancy shaped silver candle holder on it. Munching my cookie, I longed to touch the keys. Our piano was old, an upright that had clearly seen better days and whose wooden case had long ago lost its sheen, having spent years in great Aunt Matilda's gas fired living room.

I asked the new kid if she took piano lessons and she shook her head no, adding, none of us can play. Pointing her cookie in my direction Anita said, "She can play." Urged on by the new kid's mother, I took my place on the padded bench and played Swinging Lanterns. A couple more family members came into the room, so I played The Happy Farmer. They all clapped. Then I noticed the funny old father had also joined us. "Play some more little girl," he said in a thick accent. I only knew one more, so began Beethoven's Little Minuet. I was playing it through for the second time when turning, I noticed the old man was crying. What had I done?

"It's okay," assured the new kid's Mom, "Poppa hasn't heard that since we left Poland. His Mamma used to play it. But that was long ago and far away."

And so it was that I learned from my Grandpa who knew everything about our neighborhood, that the junk man's Mother had been taken away and killed by the Nazis, and that the funny looking candle holder atop their piano was called a Menorah, and that the new people to our neighborhood were Jewish.

Chapter 22

Shoe Biz

The Wagner family lived at the bottom of the street below us, and opposite the Stoutenbergs whose daughter played with Anita and me. Then she got sick with something called rheumatic fever which we'd never heard of, after which Anita and I could only visit for 5 minutes a day, or look in the window. So we quit going there and went to Winta Wagner's instead. She was younger than us and had the prettiest older sisters whom to us looked like movie stars!

Ila and Marcella would walk up the three big hills past my house and Grandpa's to the streetcar on Commercial Drive each day to go to work. They wore hats and gloves, spike heeled shoes and brightly colored dresses. They also wore red lipstick and nail polish and painted seams up the back of their tanned legs to make it look like they were wearing nylon stockings, which they weren't. With the war going on, you couldn't get nylons for love or money. That's what Mom said.

Anita and I emulated the girls every move. When we grew up we wanted to look just like them. Winta said she didn't! She just argued with them all the time. Then the mother would yell, "Vinta, shutting ze up!" At least that's what it sounded like to us. We'd wonder how the mother could look so old and plain with her paste color face and drab hair tied back in a bun as she daily scrubbed and scoured their front porch and three wide steps.

When Marcella and Ila would walk down our hill after getting off the streetcar to come home from work, teetering on their high heels, my Grandpa would look out his dining room window and laugh saying, "look at those silly girls trying to walk in those shoes, they'll break a leg!" But they didn't.

One day Ila disappeared. The neighborhood was shocked to learn she'd eloped with a handsome Marine from San Diego.

But she left most of her shoes, which Anita and I thought really decent. Winta threw them out a second floor window for us to play with. We were having a good time wearing them up and down the sidewalk until Winta's Mother caught us. After she yelled stuff in German, she did a funny thing... she tossed them all into the garbage can. Perfectly good shoes!

Chapter 23

Going For Firecrackers

Halloween to Dad meant a trip, the Saturday before October 31 to Chinatown. I suppose in many previous years before I can remember, he had gone there to purchase fire works. Or, perhaps he just began going to Chinatown to get fireworks after the first of my little brother's Norm and I were of an age to impress. Really, I don't know. But I do remember a particular pre Halloween trip on one of those gray rain soaked Vancouver Saturday afternoons to the mysterious area below Main and Hastings otherwise known as China Town.

In the 1940's to a little kid like me it seemed an area steeped in intrigue. You could safely say I was the epitome of an uptight little WASP. Sure, we'd listened to Charlie Chan on the radio, and we'd had Chinese ginger at Christmas time from little brown crockery pots sealed with pitch and tied with twine, but that was the extent of our Chinese immersion.

The only Chinese I had ever seen or spoken to were old Wah Lee and his wife Joyce who ran the green grocers at the top of Graveley Street and Commercial Drive, or the blue pajama clad fish man, straw coolee hat on his head who came to our neighborhood on Fridays, a pole hung heavy with fish over his sloping shoulders as the catch of the day dangled pungently for the housewife's approval. Because Mom was allergic to seafood we had no need of the fish-man's visits, but my Grandma next door, *(being a good Cornish lass)*, always bought a nice bit of fish from him. As I think of it, the only fish Dad ever got after becoming husband to a non-fish eating person was King Oscar's tinned sardines, or once in awhile smoked black cod at which we non-initiated fish aficionados turned up our little noses, preferring of all things, Kraft Dinner with ketchup those nights. I guess it worked out in the long run. Daddy hated the seven-minute dinner and we thought we hated fish!

The part of Vancouver's Chinatown that we stopped in was really just the fringes. Not for us the dark hidden inner alleys with names like Blood or Shanghai. Dad would park the car on Hastings Street. He'd ask if I wanted to go with him. Wimp that I was, I'd always shake my curls no. He'd walk down the sidewalk a ways, then disappear into one of those little doorways while I with my active imagination would cringe thinking I'll never ever see him again. I'd peer from the back seat window of our old dark green Ford at what seemed to be a mass of teeming humanity; all so different looking. No one was wearing hats or gloves! Most were in funny little shoes and wore strange black clothes. Some of them had long pigtails, and some of them who didn't look very clean, even spit on the pavement.

Flashing neon signs on the buildings looked peculiar and ripply in the rain, as from the moisture drizzled car window I tried to make out the names. Bamboo Gardens, Yip Sing Laundry, Ho Ying Café, and so on. I'd ask Mom, sitting in the front seat with my little brother, to read some of the names aloud. When she did, they all sounded so foreign. Could this really be my country? I'd fix my gaze on the enormous jade plant in an oversized jardiniere sitting in the dirty window of the shop opposite the curb where we were parked and wish my Daddy would reappear. Wiping condensation from the window with my coat sleeve I'd wonder what was taking him so long.

Now the rain was coming down staccato-like and the Buddha on the sign across the street seemed to be laughing at us. An old man blew his nose without using a hanky, and then adding insult to injury, fell against our car. A few people came to his aid, dragging him away just as Dad approached. I was silently crying. But there he was, with a paper package of fireworks and a grin upon his face. Turning to me he'd say, "Why would you ever think I wouldn't come back, you little silly. Now dry your tears," and he'd hand me his nicely pressed handkerchief to snivel in, adding with a voice full of boyish enthusiasm as he turned to Mom, "just wait 'til you see the great fire crackers I got this time!" She never appeared overly excited about his purchase, but then, making our trick or treat costumes was more her specialty. In her hands crepe paper became the vehicle of which dreams were made. Her years of working in Spencer's Party Shop came to the fore.

Chapter 24

Bowling For God

In our family we went to church every Sunday whether we wanted to or not. I didn't mind too much, 'cause I liked wearing my best dress and patent leather shoes. Mom said she never knew whether to get my little brother ready first or last because whatever she did he was messed up by the time we got there. Easter Sunday was my favorite time for then the iron tracery balconies that swept around the upper floor of Grandview United Church would overflow with ferns and garden flowers. The floor to ceiling organ pipes in the choir loft would embrace branches of delicate blossoms flanking a flower laden cross, while pedestals on either side of the carved communion table that usually held boring aspidistras, now supported glorious white lilies. If the perfume-sated setting didn't bring tears to your eyes, the strains from the pipe organ, choir and congregation singing "Welcome Happy Morning," would. Dad said Easter was a hay-fever sufferer's nightmare!

This church, almost at the top corner of Venables and Victoria Drive was my second home. While I knew Grandpa Phillifant had built many of the furnishings, the fact he had also built the 2-lane bowling alley sequestered beneath the church gymnasium amazed me. Who else had a grandpa who'd built a church bowling alley?

Sometimes Dad and I would escape to that sunless environ while Mom, who taught upstairs in the Sunday School Beginner's department waited for parents to pick up their offspring. Now and then it took so long for certain moms and dads to show up you'd almost think they didn't want their children back.

Meanwhile, down in the musty bowling alley, much to Dad's disdain I constantly lobbed the balls. An expert bowler, he was on a team at Marino's Bowling Alley on the drive, and had cups to prove it. But he was patient, resetting the pins time and again so I could have another try. Then Mom would come and find us and ask, "What are you two doing, bowling on a Sunday?" And Dad would reply, "we're bowling for God." This made sense to me because I already knew a verse from Ecclesiastes that I was certain said, *Remember your creator before the silver cord is loosed on the golden bowling ball.*

I knew every entrance and exit of these buildings from the secret passage behind the organ pipes, to the two floors of alcoves with folding oak doors containing obscured glass inserts, that formed a semi circle around the sanctuary. When the doors were closed over, these recessed areas became individual Sunday school classrooms. They also made great hiding spots. There were halls, stairways, minister's study, board rooms, choir room lined with wooden-doored cupboards full of black choir gowns, and a music library bursting with folders holding hundreds of anthems and music books. One room known as The Ladies Chambers, had its own carpeted platform and lectern where the women of the church met for meetings and lectures. A separate room provided equal space for men's meetings. There was a treasurer's office, a secretary's space and a room for wedding parties to gather and decide if they really wanted to get married or not. Mom told me that one time she was at a big wedding and the groom never did show up The organist kept playing his prelude music over and over until the minister finally told him to hault and then announced there'd be no wedding . So except for the bride, they just all went to the gym and ate the food anyways.

In the church basement amidst screened off furnace pipes and curtains of chintz, Mrs. Eulah Burton and her spinster sister, Miss Ruth Keast, held forth running the junior department of the Sunday School, positions they held for many years. Across the lane was the gymnasium, stage, dressing rooms, wash rooms, kitchen and Beginner's Department, and next door was a big house called the Parsonage where our minister lived and behind which sat a house so tiny it could have been a playhouse. But it wasn't. That was where Mr. Turner, the caretaker lived. One time when I was visiting, I told him it was just like a lighthouse except it wasn't surrounded by water, and he said it once was when a pipe burst!

As I sat through Sunday School and church services, choir practices and in the 1950s pipe organ lessons, the thing farthest from my mind was the possibility our church would one day become a theatre known as The Vancouver East Cultural Center.

Chapter 25

How Still We See Thee Lie

Halloween that year was not to be any fun. I didn't go trick or treating with Anita and didn't get to wear the costume Mom had made. My beloved Grandpa Phillifant who had lain, dying from cancer that week as people talked about the United Nations coming into existence, had taken his last painful breath October 30. Auntie Muriel had come home from Washington D.C. in time to see him once more, but Uncle Les was somewhere on a troop ship enroute home and arrived too late for the funeral. Grandpa hadn't lived to see his son safely returned or to perhaps trade war stories. In the basement workshop many unfinished woodworking projects sat awaiting finishing touches. They were to have been Christmas presents to us. Uncle did his best to paint and ready some, but others would remain as Grandpa had left them. I didn't like going downstairs at the Venables Street house anymore, and I didn't like playing in the glassed in potting shed under the back stairs either. It was no fun without Grandpa.

Having Uncle Les back from the war was exciting. He was engaged and going to get married. I would have a new auntie next spring.

Eleanor, the only daughter of Dr. Glen Agnew and his wife Mabel, lived on the corner of Parker Street and Victoria Drive in a large home with wide verandahs and a plant filled conservatory. She was a UBC graduate, drove her own car and worked as a secretary at Britannia High School. I didn't mind Uncle Les wanting to marry her. She always made a fuss over me and wore the most interesting clothes. Her wardrobe included things like silver colored silk stockings, velvet shoes with buckles, skirts tied with flowing taffeta sashes, a gray Persian lamb coat, purple satin cape and purses of crocodile or butter smooth suede. Sometimes she tucked a nosegay of violets into her waistband or wore oriental combs in her blonde hair. Yes, she had style. Mom and Auntie Muriel said she dressed like an old lady and who did she think she was, the Duchess of Windsor? Secretly I wished Mom had nicer clothes. Like Grandma, she always sewed everything herself. Bags of material often piled up while she wore the same best dress over and over.

Even before he had joined the army, Uncle Les would borrow me for a Sunday afternoon spent with him and Eleanor at Stanley Park where we'd visit the bears, the monkey house and the ducks. The two of them were great fun to be with and brought me presents, toys which Uncle Les had always played with first, and sometimes nearly worn out their springs. But I now felt divided in my loyalties, knowing Mom and my favorite auntie weren't keen on their brother's upcoming wedding.

Somehow we all got through that first Christmas without Grandpa Phillifant, for only 55 days had passed since his death. In the corner of the dining room of their home, stood a fresh Christmas tree. The colored tree lights with tiny hand painted celluloid shades that turned slowly as they warmed, again intrigued my little brother and me. Evergreen boughs of cedar were tucked above all the large gilt framed Victorian paintings of horses and battles and English landscapes, and the French doors between the living and dining room were again opened to make room for the extended dining room table and relatives. There would be at least twelve, but more than likely twenty with numerous first and second cousins. And that was just Mom's side of the family. We would have another gathering with the Cupit family so that Dad's kin got equal time. It seemed all that we did at Christmas was eat and eat again.

Over at Grandma and Grandpa Cupit's place on McLean Drive, the Christmas tree again held colored glass parasols in fuchsia, sapphire, emerald and gold. Wrapped with gold metallic mesh, the seven-inch embellishments glistened and gleamed. One almost expected them to magically unfurl on their very own. Auntie Lillian had sent them to her mother from New York City many Christmases ago and everyone always oohed and ahhed over them. Grandma said they were too fancy for any tree in her house, but I didn't think so. She and I played a piano duet that Boxing Day; her favorite carol... O Little Town of Bethlehem.

Christmas over, the snow now looking the color of mud lay piled against Grandview curbs as January rains pelted. School was back in session. We were still eager for the sounds of the hand rung three o'clock bell so we could hurry home and play with Christmas presents. January 5 would however be an exception. That was the day Grandma Cupit was rushed by ambulance to the Vancouver General Hospital where she died from appendicitis. What would Grandpa do now? He was still working, but didn't know anything about cooking, laundry or cleaning a house, tasks always done by Grandma.

After the funeral when we all were gathered at the cemetery I thought about the carol Grandma and I had played and sung just two weeks ago. "How still we see thee lie." And now my dear Grandma lay beneath the snow dusted earth at Ocean View just like my Grandpa. "Above thy deep and dreamless sleep the silent stars go by."

Married to my Grandma nearly 43 years, Grandpa seemed unable to find solace, repeatedly asking, "why was she took instead of me?" Auntie Lil wanted him to return to California with her and Uncle Jimmy, but he wouldn't leave his house or his old dog Shiu.

For a few weeks he either ate dinner at our house, or I took a plate of hot food next door to him at suppertime. Sometimes I stayed and ate with him, but it seemed so empty in the kitchen without Grandma bustling about. Her blue gingham apron still hung on it's hook near the pantry doorway, but the lid was closed on her piano now and never again would we smell her fresh baked loaves of bread cooling on the window sill. Grandpa just kept crying.

Mom and Dad decided he needed a little budgie to keep him company, so a cage and little blue/green bird were added to his kitchen. He said he didn't want it, but made a fuss over the bird called Perky when he thought no one noticed. Then he retired from work as a bricklayer and seemed only to sit smoking his pipe and reading the daily newspaper. On Fridays, dressed in suit, tie and best hat, he walked the three blocks up the hill to the Royal Bank on Commercial Drive, picked up a few groceries at the Safeway or Rays Supermarket and returned home. Something was going to have to be done. He needed a housekeeper.

One Monday that April when I came running through the door from school I was told little Norm and I would be going to spend a week with Grandma Phillifant. It would be Easter holidays. What fun! I loved going to Grandma's where I could sleep in one of the twin beds snuggled beneath a green and gold satin quilt, my favorite doll Peggy by my side. And that Tuesday, April 16 when the phone rang at Grandma's Dad told us that we had a new baby brother! William Henry, named after his two grandfathers's had been added to our family. I was not terribly thrilled to know I now had two little brothers with which to share my room. But it was a great Easter, for after attending church with Grandma we went back to her house to find baskets crammed with more chocolate eggs than we'd seen or imagined during the long war years. We'd been thoroughly spoiled by Auntie Muriel, Grandma, and Uncle Les who had purchased treats from a downtown chocolate shop. A few days later we returned home as Mom and baby William who she said the Easter bunny had delivered, arrived home from the hospital.

For a week we were looked after by Great Aunt Matilda, or Aunt Til as we called her. She cooked suppers for us and did a bit of light housekeeping before returning nightly to her West End apartment. It was around this time that someone came up with the idea she'd be the perfect housekeeper for Grandpa. And shortly thereafter, all arrangements made, she moved in to his house and took over the back bedroom for herself.

Aunt Til was not a gourmet cook. In fact, she liked to say she was a plain cook. But an obstacle to any kind of cooking loomed in Grandpa's kitchen... a gas stove! She was deathly afraid of it. An old gray porcelain clad stove with a top warming oven, it had many peculiarities. The levers for each jet had to be tilted just at the right angle and then the jets lit by matches. One afternoon just before suppertime, we kids were playing in our back yard when there was the loudest explosion we'd ever heard. At first we thought it was the gas tanks! But no, it had come from the other direction. The bang brought Mom running from our kitchen along with several neighbors. And there on Grandpa's back porch was a tearful Aunt Til wiping her face on her apron and saying, "I could have been killed!" Indeed she probably could have been, for the large kitchen window had been blown right out of the house. Shards of glass now littered the next door yard of the Olyinsky's

Chapter 26

Weddings, Dancing and Dawdlings

When she married Uncle Les in the living room of her parent's home, my new aunt, Eleanor, wore a rather prim blue lace gown. It was the first wedding I'd ever been to, and I was disappointed because I thought she'd look like the brides gowned and veiled in white, pictured in the social pages of the newspapers. She didn't even have a bridesmaid. It wasn't a very long ceremony, and after the cake had been cut and everybody ate, there was nothing more to do, so the bride and groom left. Dad and I went home and told Mom all about it because she couldn't attend since she had our new baby to look after. When I told her about the blue dress she just said, "older brides don't wear white!"

After they'd had a honeymoon in San Francisco, where there were cable cars and sea lions, the newlyweds moved into an apartment in an old West End home on Denman Street where I was invited for dinner along with Grandma and her brother. I was enthralled by the apartment. There were lots of interesting pieces of oriental and European antique furniture which Grandma said was nice to look at, but uncomfortable to sit upon. Instead of logs and a fire in the fireplace, an open parasol bearing hand painted blossoms filled the opening. We ate at a round dining room table set upon a platform with drapes and swags behind it. Amidst potted palms, a couple of pillars held crystal candelabra. It was rather like being in a stage set. This was the first time I'd dined by candlelight and the first time I'd been served Waldorf salad to begin a meal. Grandma's brother, whom we called Uncle, took all the walnuts out of his salad and left them on the side of his plate, muttering something about "blinkin' nuts." But I ate mine because Mom had told me to be polite and eat everything even if I didn't like it. I didn't know what some of the food was, but I ate every bit so they would invite me again. Aunt Eleanor was wearing a peacock blue cheong-sam which I thought looked prettier than her wedding dress, and Uncle Les, a dinner jacket. Yes, they had panache.

Our brother Bill with his dark brown eyes and hair wasn't the only new addition to the family that spring of 1946. Auntie Muriel, now working days as a private secretary at B.A. Oil and editing a sports magazine in the evenings needed some form of transportation. A maroon colored Chevrolet club coupe straight out of the downtown showroom was her choice and she paid cash for it. Then, as she didn't know how to drive, her cousin who worked at B.C. Telephone on Seymour drove it back to Venables Street for her. She then set about taking driving lessons from Dad who had the patience of Job.

The idea of anyone having a sparkling new car that had never belonged to another person was unheard of amongst our family members. After all the hardships of war, this was an amazing acquisition, especially for a single woman.

The first weekend the car was hers, Auntie Muriel decided we should drive to Blaine and buy Hershey's chocolate bars. They were unavailable in Canada. And so, with Dad driving, Muriel and Mom rode in the front seat with young Norm, baby Billy and I cradled by cushions occupying the back jump seat. I was excited to be entering the United States for the first time and as we passed the Spanish styled buildings at the border I figured in no time we'd be in

California where my cousins lived. Of course I was wrong. We just had time to buy chocolate bars, a tin of Edgeworth's tobacco for Grandpa and then turn around and head back to B.C. Without freeways it was a long trip.

In time Auntie Muriel learned to drive her car and would take me on exploration trips. Sometimes we just went somewhere and shopped. Beautiful shoes were her weakness. Paper dolls were mine. When her best friend from Washington married an airforce man at Canadian Memorial Church, I attended with Grandma because Muriel was a bridesmaid. It was my first big formal wedding and when the bridal party exited the church and walked beneath an honor guard formed by uniformed airforce men, boy was I impressed!

By September that year all family adjustments had been made. Aunt Til was looking after Grandpa which meant he was less of a concern, and at Grandma Phillifant's, Uncle was keeping the house and garden in order. He didn't relish his new role. Puttering and deadheading in the garden and caring for all those bloomin' goldfish and the blinkin' pond were not his cup of tea. Where my Grandpa had thrived on such events as the opening of the first varicolored crocus or the birth of a hybrid rose, Uncle could care less. But he would do his best.

With us living next door to Grandpa Cupit, it was Dad that had to cut his father's lawns, clean the chimney, clear the snow and maintain the outward appearance of that address as well as ours. Although Dad would paint our place every few years, his father's house would never see another coat of paint. Grandpa wouldn't spend the money, saying it didn't matter now that Grace was gone. He wouldn't walk his dog Shiu anymore, so one of us had to take on that responsibility.

Anita and I were in grade three and adored Mrs. Taylor, our teacher. I was still going to piano lessons once a week. It was a long walk each Friday afternoon following school. Mom would push baby Billy in his carriage with Norm riding on one side of the buggy and me trailing alongside. All those hills and three kids to care for as she walked the 15 blocks there and back showed real dedication on her part. And then for some reason she decided I should also take dancing classes. Phyllis Thomson taught highland and tap. Because we weren't Scottish and Dad envisioned his daughter becoming a second Ginger Rogers, I was put in tap. Phyllis's studio was in the same general area as my piano teacher's home, so it meant another long walk to and from lessons on another day of the week. Dad bought me a pair of the most beautiful white leather tap shoes and began playing his old gramophone records for me to practice to. Lullaby of Broadway was one of his favorites, along with The Continental. Both a little out of my league, I practiced my slap pickup down down diligently to The Parade of the Wooden Soldiers. Even though I took part in a few reviews, I was to be a dancing disappointment to him. A couple of years later they changed me over to The Hyslop Dancing School which was more expensive and being above Nanaimo Street, meant he had to drive me to and from lessons every Saturday. In the end, any thoughts of my having a career in tap were abandoned. Tickling the ivories was more my forte.

When I was finally considered old enough to walk to and from my piano lessons alone, I often dawdled enroute home.

In the 20 hundred block of Napier Street just off Victoria Drive, stood the red brick Catholic Church, St. Francis of Assisi. It looked stark to me, but in contrast, on the opposite side of the street, the walled in Franciscan convent with tree shaded lawns had appeal. I'd stop at the big iron gates, rattling them to see if they were locked. They always were, and I wondered if the people inside were locked in, or I locked out? It was so peacefully quiet and green in those grounds. Resting my music case by the garden wall, I'd watch the nuns strolling about while reading from their books, seemingly oblivious to my peering eyes. What were they doing? One time, since he and Grandma lived only blocks away and would know, I asked Uncle about them. He gruffly replied, "they're Dogans and they're reading the daily offices. Not allowed out except to go to mass!"

What was mass? I knew Anita went to mass, but she sure wasn't locked in, and when I asked her if she was a dogan, she said she didn't even know what that meant but it was probably a bad word.

If I continued my lone adventures skipping along Victoria Drive past Dr. Agnew's corner house with its fern-filled solarium, I'd come upon a private hospital, which on warm sun-filled Friday afternoons warranted a brief stop. On such days, the wheel chair patients would be outside with their nurses, getting a breath of air. A big terrace shaded beneath great green striped canvas awnings sheltered others still in their beds. The gardens were attractive and I'd try to envision the old building minus its pathetic inhabitants. In my imagination I could see the place as a small palace. Once when I told Mom that, she said, "some palace, it's more like a prison!"

On other piano lesson days when upon whim, my route took me down Napier Street to Salisbury Drive, I'd pass an imposing structure at 1036 known as Glen Hospital. It too was for invalids and people needing round the clock care. The turreted mansion had once boasted a much more romantic sounding name, Kurajong, and Dad said it had been the private estate of J.J. Miller, the founder and first president of the P.N.E.

To me, the word Kurajong spilled off the tongue sounding every bit as beautiful as the pink blossomed trees it was named for. I asked Mom why it got changed to plain old Glen Hospital and she said, "because some people just have no imagination!" Then I asked why our house didn't have a name and Mom said because it wasn't big enough. I knew she was right because out on Southwest Marine Drive where we sometimes took a Sunday drive there stood Spanish mansions with names like Casa Loma. A white pillared and porticoed estate in Shaughnessy, known as The Hollies was as big as a hotel. Dad's cousin Mabel had her wedding reception there and my cousin Marilyn and I had a wonderful time exploring its many rooms. We especially liked the exotic black and white aptly named Zebra Room.

Somehow it didn't seem fair that in order to be denoted, one's house had to be of a certain size. That night, after I'd said my prayers and snuggled beneath my covers, I decided to give our house a name. I thought about all the plants that grew in our front garden and decided the blue lace-cap hydrangea by the front steps was my favorite. Unknown to anyone but me, our little bungalow with it's leaded glass windows became LaceCap. In my mind I could actually see the sign hanging above the front door while a maid opened it and said, "welcome to LaceCap. Lady Joan is in the blue room."

Chapter 27

Goodbye Shiu, Hello Buffalo Park

Old Shiu, blind, deaf and mostly toothless was gone. I had come home from school just in time to see him being led on a rope towards the dog catchers truck. Silently and showing no resistance the once proud, now aged Chinese Chow was lifted into the truck and the wire screened partition like a cell door snapped closed. "Grandpa!" I called, "where's Shiu going?" In my heart I knew the answer, for Shiu had been sick. We'd all seen the pound man and his notorious vehicle picking up hapless strays and used up pets. We kids hated him. Some of the boys in the neighborhood used to throw rocks at his truck accomplishing little aside from upsetting the captive canines while setting every dog within earshot to howling and barking. Grandpa turned away from me and walked back inside his yard, closed the gate and went into his basement. As the truck pulled away I began to run after it, but knew it was futile. Anita ran after me and then we both sat on the curb and cried. I vowed never to speak to my Grandpa ever again. But of course I did.

On warm autumn days when we had nothing else to do, and to give Mom a rest, Anita and I would offer to take my new baby brother for a walk in his carriage. He was a happy, chubby little boy with an easygoing personality. Now that he could sit up in the buggy and look at the passing scene old ladies would often stop, peer at him and say, "oh what a lovely child, just look at those dimples!" He'd smile back, completely charming them. We were only supposed to walk him around the immediate neighborhood, or one square block, but for some reason that day decided to do an extended stroll all the way out to Buffalo Park. Why it was called that I've no idea, for to my knowledge there never were any buffalo to be seen. The park now as extinct as it's namesake was away out at the end of Commercial Drive. We were not supposed to be on Commercial Drive. We walked and walked, and then our once happy faced baby got tired of the whole scenario and clenching his little fists began to fuss. No matter what we did he wouldn't stop, so Anita who always had money went into a small store and bought him a chocolate ice cream cone. It did the trick. He loved it.

Heading back home along the Drive we had to pass Davies Plumbing and Sheet Metal where Dad worked and as luck would have it, he happened to be outside loading tools into the trunk of his car. Upon encountering Anita and I gliding by with his chocolate covered son, he did a double take. We were duly chastised, my now frantic Mother telephoned and then, the buggy and we were loaded into the car and driven home. My punishment for baby napping was having to fold his daily supply of clean Curity diapers every afternoon and not being allowed out to play. Not bad if it hadn't been for the fact that was the very week Anita got a brand new balloon tired bicycle from her rich relatives in Chicago.

Chapter 28

Simply Marble-Less

By the time another year had left its indelible imprint on our lives, my brother Norm had undergone more surgery done to erase the scars of a hair lip. He entered grade one.

Now, when Anita and I went to school we had him accompanying us in the morning and at noon when we went home for lunch break. It was an awesome responsibility for someone was always confronting him about his scars and asking what happened to his face? On the one hand I felt obliged to defend him while on the other, I wished he'd get lost. It seemed he was always in trouble.

On the grounds at Woodland Elementary, the sexes were segregated. Two large sheds with dirt floors served as rainy day play areas. There was no school gym. If the sun came out, the girls could skip rope or play jacks on a concrete pad near the school while the boys over on the far side of the building played marbles or a game using waxed paper milk bottle caps. There was no playground equipment. Other city schools may have been better equipped, but we were East Enders, and this was 1947.

In spring, softball generally considered a boy's sport was played on the small field. The girls could watch, but seldom had a team of their own, a fact that suited me fine having determined even then the athletic life was not for me.

Norman collected marbles. Beautiful marbles. Not today's kind manufactured of cheap colored glass, but REAL marbles. A lot of them had come from Dad's boyhood collection and others had been willed to him by male relatives or friends instructed by their wives to get rid of such childish attachments. Unable to toss them into infinity with reckless abandon, these males felt that Norm, quiet little fellow who'd just been through another delicate operation, would love their marbles! And he did. He now had so many he housed them in large round metal tobacco tins which our pipe smoking Grandpa provided. Sometimes when he sorted them at the foot of his bed, they kind of got away on him and he'd drop a can on the second story hardwood floor. Five hundred marbles and steelies suddenly hitting a wooden floor can certainly give you a jolt if you're directly beneath them. And when some of them find their way through the metal heat register gaining speed as they cascade and spiral through two floors of metal duct work to the basement furnace... well! One time Mom dropped Dad's freshly baked custard pie right on the kitchen floor, breaking the pyrex pie plate and rendering the four eggs pie useless.

After this, six-year old Norm had his marbles canned, confiscated, and carefully carried to the basement. Someone suggested a nice quiet hobby like matchbook collecting, but he'd already set Dad's bench on fire twice. So that was out.

Chapter 29

My Brothers The Cross-Dressers

The Dionne Quintuplets had been born back in 1934, but at our house they were reborn off and on every few years when someone needed a quick costume.

Mom had sewn the five white adult sized baby dresses and frilly bonnets for masquerade costumes. Now sequestered in a metal trunk under the eaves, they lay neatly folded incongruously side by side with other of her creations including a black lace mantilla and red Spanish dress, a blue spangled mermaid tail and pink ruffled hoop skirted gown that made Strauss waltzes ripple through your mind. Except for the quintuplet dresses, each outfit had a corresponding costume for a male. When Mom had gone to a party as a senorita, Dad had been a gaucho, when she had been a mermaid, he'd been King Neptune, and so on. Rainy days were never boring at our place because we could always play dress-up with wonderful costumes.

My parents never went to masquerades anymore. Aside from the fact they now had three kids, Mom had gone onto other creative endeavors. In her spare time she was doing window displays for McLeans Stationery Store at the top of the lane between Graveley and 1st Avenue next to Cooks Corner, a small convenience store. An old couple named the Hoggs owned and operated the shop and were trying to promote a shipment of Cupie dolls, the latest craze. For every Hallmark occasion that year Mom did a window scene using the chubby toys. For Valentine's, dressed like a little bride and groom, they were posed walking over a satin-covered bridge which ran through a crepe paper frilled heart. At St. Patrick's they were wee leprechauns peeking through a gold and green harp, at graduation, outfitted in black capes and mortarboards, they carried tiny rolled up diplomas. In some ways these 12 inch dolls with impish grins and points atop their heads became part of our family. As sales soared I was given my own cupie which I named Rose!

With this added responsibility of window dressing on Mom's mind, and the fact she had offered to paint scenery and organize the church fall concert, as Halloween approached, our costumes didn't materialize. And so, the three of us, plus friends Anita and Linda were put into quintuplet dresses. Norm didn't want to be a girl, and didn't pull it off properly because he refused to wear the bonnet and put a jacket over his dress. But our little brother Billy made an adorable baby girl. When we arrived at Grandpa's back door and called out, "trick or treat,"he took one look and gasped, disgusted to see two of his grandsons dressed like girls. Aunt Til, on the other hand laughed her head off. "Oh tiddly dum dum, will you have a look at this," she snickered. Then slapping her knees in delight she bent down and gave both boys kisses and apples, but ignored us girls. It went like that, more or less, at every house we visited that evening. When we finally took little Billy back home I think we were sorry he had to go back to being a boy. Norm vowed never to leave the house ever again. But he did, when his candy ran out.

Chapter 30

Another Groom, Another June

Auntie Muriel had resigned from her job at B.A. Oil and was now free-lancing full time and making good money as a writer. She was also dating a divorced middle-aged man with a 14-year-old son. They had met at the Royal Vancouver Yacht Club when she was writing a story for a yachting magazine.

J.T. as he liked to be called had a small sailboat, an old yellow MG and an ex-wife who purportedly dressed like a man. Being 1947 and Vancouver, the latter was not revealed for many years. When Auntie Muriel and J T became engaged, Grandma was not overjoyed. There was a stigma attached to divorced people. It would be difficult to explain to family members and friends. I think she hoped the whole affair would blow over. But Auntie Muriel was now in her mid-thirties and didn't savor the idea of living at home and caring for her mother and uncle as they aged. Marriage, even to a fast-talking, balding 50-year-old with few assets, seemed preferable. And so she had accepted his ring with a diamond so tiny Mom's cousin said you needed a magnifying glass to see it.

Trying to do the correct thing, Grandma invited the prospective groom's family for Sunday tea along with members of our clan. We were all gathered in her pale blue and cream living room when the entourage pulled up and we heard them clattering up the many stairs to the front porch. Was this some kind of joke? All the men were wearing Stetsons. The father referred to as Boss, was a rotund fellow with a huge cigar in one hand. The younger son known as Tannie had curly hair and was soft spoken with perfectly manicured hands. He was a bachelor and didn't say much, but seemed very nice. A skinny fast talking brother in law visiting from the U.S. had a twitching eye and was the other adult male in the group along with J.T.'s 14 year old son who looked extremely nervous. We were told he attended a private boy's school in Vancouver and was wearing his school uniform. My brothers weren't impressed and eyed him suspiciously from behind Grandma's aspidistras. Because he was a boy, I refused to acknowledge him. Nor would my third cousin Ruthie, who they kept pointing out was about the same age as him.

The mother, a biggish rather jolly woman was decked out in a huge flowered picture hat and many pieces of chunky jewellery. A daughter, who appeared to be looking forward in vain, to afternoon cocktails and her snobby, 16 year old offspring completed the group. They were all very loud and called everybody honey! To say they didn't fit in with our group would be an understatement. Grandma did her best as she poured tea from her bone china teapot with the yellow roses, and offered tiny cakes, breads and tarts. I looked them over and thought, aha, so this is what a family with a divorced person in it looks like.

After we'd been as nice as possible for as long as possible, we kids went outside to Grandma's back yard where Norm tried to show off by walking through the fish pond on the stepping stones. Our little brother Billy followed and fell in. This was not good. He was wearing cream colored short pants and sweater, and new white boots. After that we went straight home. Dad looked happy about it. Mom though, anything but pleased, complained all the way home that they were just going to talk about the wedding plans and now she'd miss it all, and what on earth could her sister Muriel be thinking of marrying into a family like that?

When Auntie Muriel married she had envisioned her long-dreamed about church wedding would take place at Grandview United just like my Mom and Dad's way back in 1936. But now, because she was marrying a divorced man, a church wedding was out of the question. Nor could she wear white. Marrying a divorcee in those times definitely had rules.

There's an old saying, "when the world wearies, and society ceases to satisfy, there is always the garden." And so it was amidst the forgiving and fragrant larkspur, lilies and June roses of her late father's beloved Venables Street garden that she was wed in a blue moiré taffeta gown. I was her only attendant, a rather chunky 10 year old in shell pink taffeta.

At the reception in Grandma's very Victorian dining room, the mood was more akin to the follow up of a funeral than a joyous event. Grandma wore gray and a pained expression most of the afternoon. Uncle Les was the photographer, but Aunt Eleanor chose only to attend the ceremony, slipping out through the back garden gate and escaping to her car as soon as the couple were pronounced man and wife.

Mom who was 6 months pregnant with her 4th child was remarkably subdued, spending most of her time in Grandma's pantry washing tea cups and replenishing sandwich trays while Dad patrolled my two little brothers, keeping them well away from the notorious fish pond and the temptations of the garden with it's tantalizing raspberry patch, grape arbors and ripening pea vines.

Quiet clusters of mostly disapproving relatives made small talk and looked rather pityingly in Auntie Muriel's direction. One of the old aunties was overheard suggesting she should have married the groom's brother for he was much younger and better looking, to which Aunt Til replied, "but he's one of those mamma's boys!"

At every opportunity I walked across the polished floors or outside on the large front porch just to twirl and hear the rustling of this, my first long gown. Colonial bouquet in hand, I swished past my second cousins, Stanley and Ronnie, both a couple of years my senior. Seated on hard wooden chairs, their only entertainment lay in trying to trip me or snatch at my tissue paper stiffened back bustle. I'd give them my best haughty look and whisper, "hah, you missed!" They could hardly wait 'til I entered Junior High so they could get even.

Chapter 31

A Sliver Of Summer

Summer afternoon, summer afternoon: to me those have always been the two most beautiful words in the English language said Henry James.

And now that school was out 62 blissful days lay ahead. Anita and I spent most of those daylight hours together playing movie stars with our Betty Grable cutouts or, at the other extreme, making trails in the bush across the back lane with a neighbor kid a few years older than us.

Margaret-Ann was a tomboy. Her mother worked and was gone all day leaving Margaret-Ann in the care of her older brother, a pimply faced boy with horned rimmed spectacles who mostly ignored her, spending his time doing science experiments in his bedroom. Every once in awhile there'd be an explosion followed by a putrid smell. Once he blew up a bunch of eggs in their claw footed bathtub. Wow, what a mess.

That she had a working mother and no supporting father was in itself unusual. It hadn't always been like that. For awhile they had been a quiet family of four living in the tomato red house, sharing the shade and fall cleanup of the large maple tree sidling Dad's garage. But then, their travelling salesman father who always dressed in silk suits and wore a diamond pinkie ring, got a new car. It was a bullet nose Studebaker and looked the same viewed from the front or back. The neighborhood had no sooner gotten over that shock, making jokes about whether he was coming or going, when he and his Studebaker left town forever with another woman!

Margaret-Ann formed a club. To become a member and be able to partake of the trails in the bush where you could eat wild berries and spit the pits wherever you liked or swing from the tire suspended from a spindly alder, screaming alley alley oop at the top of your lungs, you first had to be initiated. There was a two-part test. You first had to pick up a live worm! Being squeamish, I failed that one right away.

On most summer evenings before stillness had fallen and the crickets in the ditches had begun their serenade, the neighborhood gang played baseball on McLean Drive. The game went on until the last kid had been called home for bath and bed. Margaret-Ann said that since I'd failed the live worm part, I could be a club member if, when my Mom called me, instead of taking the normal back lane route home I would cut through Mrs. Findlay's yard and climb the cedar fence separating it from my own back yard. What could I do? I had to agree. Everyone else had done the worm thing including tiny blonde haired Linda, my nemesis from up the street, who although a year younger than me could play the piano better and had gold stars galore on every page. My music books bore comments like, "play the music the way Chopin wrote it, not your interpretation!"

The first time the bases were loaded and it was my turn at bat, Mom's voice sounded, sailing over the clotheslines calling me home. Rather relieved to get out of the game because my bat rarely made contact with anything other than air, I knew Margaret-Ann's assigned route lay ahead.

To cut through Mrs. Findlay's yard was not as simple as it sounds. A middle-aged widow with jet-black hair and rimmed eyeglasses, she was housekeeper to her older bald-headed brother, also widowed and his good-looking 17-year-old son Nickie. Mrs. Findlay yelled at everybody except her cats all the time. Her accent was thick and most of her threats aimed at us kids were unintelligible for she and her brother were from Syria. She would scream and gesture wildly with the broom she always seemed to have at hand. Her old brother who worked as a night watchman and slept during the days was called Mr. Hassie, and some of the bolder kids dropped the "H" taunting him as he walked up his front steps.

Curly headed Nick had an athletic build and liked to wile away time doing chin-ups between the posts of their ground level clothesline until his aunt would shriek, "Nickie, Nickie!" in an ear splitting pitch. He'd usually ignore her until she'd open the squeaky screen door and whack him with her broom. Although Nick didn't go to a school in our area and didn't play ball with us, he sometimes watched from his front verandah. When he did, Margaret-Ann got extra bossy just so he'd notice her.

Despite the fact my mother would never strike me with a broom, I knew when she called I had to immediately head home, and so I raced up over the ditch and headed along the wobbly wooden plank pathway at the side of Mrs. Findlay's yard. I managed to sashay through her cabbages and beets and onto the top fence board just as she came out screaming, causing Nick to look out a window at me. One leg up, I slipped receiving a huge wooden sliver in my behind before falling unceremoniously into my own back yard. Letting out a wail, I ran crying, up the stairs and into the kitchen. Mom took one look and said, "that's a nasty sliver, it's got to come out." I screamed and protested as she called Dad from the basement. How embarrassing, having to bend over and lift the skirt of my dress. He just said, "hmm, tsk, tsk," in his usual quiet tone and shook his head as Mom produced tweezers, needle, Mercurochrome and bandages from her St. John's Ambulance kit. I refused to cooperate. Mom yelled, "don't be such a boob, people in the war lost arms and legs with less noise!" I wondered how she knew, but really didn't care at that point for now the entire ball team had squeezed onto our back verandah. My little brothers were giggling, and horror of horrors, Nick had come over the fence to see what happened. I insisted the cedar sliver be left where it was; I'd get used to the pain. But no... they laid me on the kitchen table, face down and operated. How humiliating.

The next day Margaret-Ann said I could be in her club as soon as I could sit down.

Chapter 32

Dad's Model A

Back in 1936 when Dad married Mom he owned two cars. Being a practical man, he soon realized keeping a wife and one car on the road was enough during the Depression, so he gave his canvas-topped 1926 Model T to a younger brother. He kept his 1929 Ford Tudor Sedan which he'd purchased in almost new condition way back in 1930.

The bottle-green-colored car had taken my parents to Seattle and Vancouver Island for their honeymoon, and transported Dad to and from work at cousin George's plumbing and sheet metal shop on Commercial Drive. It carried them to the Piggly Wiggly for groceries on Saturdays and to church every Sunday. They took summer trips to the Cariboo on the narrow white-knuckle Fraser Canyon route, pre-Christmas jaunts to Lulu Island to get us a pine tree, and so many Sunday afternoon drives around Stanley Park, the car could have been put on automatic pilot.

When I came along in 1938, the trusty Ford carried me, relatively speaking, to and from my birthplace, Grace Hospital. During the ensuing years it took us on yearly holidays to the family camp at Crescent Beach where Dad once tried to teach Mom how to drive.

She hit a tree. End of lessons. The car with its hefty bumper was fine, but Mom was never permitted to take the wheel again.

Nearly every Saturday morning, if Dad didn't have a job at the shop that day, he washed and polished the car, lovingly buffing the chrome headlamps, grill, door latches and oval enclosed Ford insignia. He'd clean the ripply glass that covered the 21-21 candle power lamp bulbs, the spokes that centered those thin tires, the spare tire mounted on the rear, and the front roof and drip moldings that always reminded me of a big visor. Mom called them the car's eyebrows.

And then it was time for the interior, which I was allowed to polish. Hawes lemon oil which was rubbed on all the wood grain parts of the dash, and sometimes when I became overly enthusiastic, the steering wheel, became part of the familiar scent of our car.

Near the back lane of our house stood the boxy double garage with flat roof, which had a section of removable planks in the floorboards. Periodically, when the car needed servicing, Dad would lift the heavy boards and climb beneath the vehicle to do maintenance and repairs. I'd kneel and watch as he crawled down into the hollow pit beneath the car, sometimes muttering about the darned neighbor's cats having been in there again. As his helper up top, I'd hand the various tools down to him. We were a team.

The sturdy little Model A had seen us through the war years when it's headlamps had to be covered with only a slit of light being permitted to shine forth during blackouts. And when gas rationing was in effect and leisurely drives around the park were curtailed, it sat patiently waiting for better days.

When the war was over and our family had grown to include my brothers, Dad decided, rather wistfully, it was time for another car. He cleaned it up for the last time all by himself. I was heartbroken that "our car" was leaving forever to be replaced by a Chevrolet. No matter how nice the new car was going to be, I just knew it wouldn't ever be as good as the old Ford. I sat in the familiar grey upholstered back seat with my favorite doll for one last time before Dad drove it away and sold it for $100. I tearfully vowed never to ride in the new car, ever! Of course, I eventually got over the loss, but through the years Dad would sometimes sigh and say, "I should have kept the old Ford, it was one in a million!"

Chapter 33

Two For The Lougheed

The only good thing about another brother was the fact I finally got my very own bedroom. Early that October, Edward John, immediately tagged Ted, was born. Our house on Graveley Street was beginning to show stretch marks as Dad began building a room in the basement and moved our dining room furniture down there. Now if we had any big family dinners with extra guests, we'd have to carry everything down the basement stairs, in order to dine 'round the old oak table with extra leaves that had once been Aunt Til's. Following the Christmas that Mom fell down those very stairs while carrying the wooden case containing our silver cutlery, dinners served below became few and far between.

Although closet-less at that point, what had been our pretty little main floor dining room just off the kitchen, became my parent's bedroom and I, now aged 10 and being the only girl, was given their upstairs front bedroom. It was my own little domain with closet, built-in cupboards and niches under the sloping eaves. As Dad liked to say, it had a place for everything and everything in its place. I also had the best view, looking out across the square block of bush towards Grouse Mountain and The Lions for which our district had first been named Grand View! My old Victorian cast iron bed that had come from Grandma's house was modernized when Dad built hollow plywood slipcovers, painted white, to hide the ornate curly-cues of the head and foot. Such details were then out of vogue.

A painting of an austere looking Christ in princely robes, wearing a crown of thorns, and carrying a lighted lantern as he knocks on a door, hung in the hallway separating my room from that of my brothers. The eyes seemed to gaze at us every time we went in or out. It had been a house- warming gift from Grandma Phillifant.

My brothers would live dormitory style; bed, chest, bed, chest, bed, chest. No frills. After all they were boys! But first Uncle, who was a painter and plasterer, would be called upon to do some decorating.

He never owned a car, so Dad would pick him and his equipment up before going to work himself at 8 a.m. Fascinated, we kids watched as Uncle mixed a powder called Vello into large metal containers with a big wooden paddle. I suppose it was blended with water to obtain just the right tint and consistency. There was none of this business of choosing a scheme from paint chips and color coordinating everything. Nor were we children consulted as to preferences. Until I was 18 and coerced Mom into a then trendy chartreuse green and flamingo pink scheme, our living room would remain buff, my room and that of my parents would be pastel peach or pale aqua and the boys room, sand colored which seemed almost to be a combination of the latter. The woodwork always stayed dark.

Uncle was never expected to paint the kitchen or bathroom. Dad did these rooms, working around our meals and other needs, using enamel which tended to last many years and could be scrubbed when necessary, like the time Mom was cooking a ham in our new presto cooker and it blew up, depositing the juicy cottage roll on our ceiling.

That fall the Lougheed Highway opened, and along with many other Vancouverites, we took our first Sunday afternoon drive on it's smooth asphalt in Dad's metallic green four door 1939 Chevrolet with what would later be classified as suicide doors. Unlike cars manufactured since then, the rear doors of that model opened towards the front doors of the vehicle, creating a suction-like effect if opened while travelling.

Still wearing his Sunday best, Dad was driving and Mom sitting in the front passenger seat was holding our new baby brother Ted, wrapped in blankets and christening shawl. There were no such things as infant seats or seat belts in those days. Norm, Billy and I were riding in the back seat, and as I recall, punching one another and fooling around when suddenly, Billy fell against the car door handle causing the door to swing open. He went flying out onto the Lougheed Highway as I screamed, "Daddy, Daddy...," before being sucked out after him.

Lying in gravel and hurting all over, I looked up from the ditch to see row upon row of vehicles stopped and people coming towards me. My knees were bleeding and the dress I'd worn to Sunday school that morning was torn and bloody. I had gravel in my mouth. Then I saw someone carrying my little brother to Dad. A stranger asked if I could walk. We were taken to a farmhouse just off the highway where a nurse from one of the cars wrapped our wounds in borrowed towels and linen handkerchiefs before we were put back in Dad's car and driven to a doctor's office above a shop on Commercial Drive. Three-year-old Billy had a head injury, which was cleaned, stapled and bandaged. I had only suffered abrasions. I don't remember too much else about that day other than the fact Billy went into convulsions that night and a doctor came to our house. Why he was never taken to a hospital is beyond me, but perhaps his injuries weren't life threatening. In those days hospitals were used as a last resort. It was a long time before we ever took another Sunday afternoon drive, and until we got another car, the doors in the back seat were tied shut with shoelaces.

Chapter 34

Off To The Cariboo

The Cariboo and Clinton, B.C. seemed a million miles away. That was where Mom and Dad's dear friends the Sutherlands lived. Cam was the Government Agent. His wife Ethel had been amongst Mom's best friends forever. Indeed, Grandma Phillifant and Ethel's Mother, Mabel Rhead, who hailed from the U.S. had known each other for many years before establishing themselves in Vancouver's Grandview district, where Mabel, her blacksmith husband Walter and their offspring lived in the 1200 block of Woodland Drive. Attending the same church as the Phillifants and Cupits, their families grew up together. Then in the 1920's when a young Cam Sutherland came from his family's farm in Ashcroft to attend high school in the city he boarded with the Rheads and of course met Ethel.

After marriage, they had moved from Grandview to Clinton, and their children came along in birth order more or less at the same time as we did. This meant another generation of friends.

Dad, who had traveled to the Cariboo before marrying Mom, and again with her to visit Cam and Ethel in 1937, loved that part of B.C. Maybe it brought out a longing for wide open spaces and the simple life of a cowboy, so different to being stuck in the back of his Uncle's shop on Commercial Drive pressing out sheet metal for furnace pipes. Anyhow, for a few years we would travel that treacherous trail of road known as the Fraser Canyon route to spend some vacation time visiting the clan Sutherland.

The house they lived in was a big old wooden two-story sun-faded structure surrounded by sagebrush-strewn property and gentle hills, punctuated here and there with jack pines. There were several outbuildings and a decaying barn. Petrified cow pies and the odd animal skull left to bleach in the sun gave evidence there had been herds at some time. It was a kids' paradise.

Elsie Kay, named after two of her aunts, had naturally curly brown hair and blue eyes framed with long lashes. She was a few months my junior and her two little brothers, blond haired Don and young Cliff, nicknamed Biff, were the ages of two of my three brothers. It was August when the Sutherlands, who had visited their many relatives in Vancouver, asked if I'd like to travel back to Clinton with them for a holiday. My parents and brothers would drive up to collect me in a week's time. An adventure!

Cam who drove a wood-sided station wagon, was tall with sandy hair and wore glasses. He, blond-haired vivacious Ethel and their kids arrived early that August morning from the Rhead's Woodland Drive residence to pick up me and my suitcase for the journey. We would travel as far as Ashcroft the first day, staying at Cam's sister Elsie Kincaid's farm for supper and the night.

In those days before air-conditioned vehicles and freeways it was a long hot trip which didn't really matter to kids having a great time enroute singing songs like Ninety-nine Bottles Of Beer On The Wall, over and over again, or playing games like I Spy With My Little Eye. None of our shenanigans seemed to phase easygoing Cam. We had a couple of picnics by rivers edge before swinging over to the dry, dusty little town of Ashcroft on the Thompson River where the Kincaid farm nestled beneath apple trees.

Elsie and husband Sam welcomed us and while dinner cooked, Elsie Kay and I took a walk on the wild side, down the railroad tracks towards town, only to be chased away by a drunk wielding a broken bottle who scared the wits out of us. I'd never seen anybody inebriated before, nor had I ever seen a native person. The rest of that hot sticky evening was spent secure inside the farm house even though it meant singing hymns around the parlor organ with the boy cousins and a couple of farm hands, for Elsie was the local church organist. It was in Ashcroft that I first became aware of the beauty of crickets chirping in the still of the night or wakened to a crowing rooster at sunrise. This was the first time I'd ever been away from home, but now, here I was miles away in a strange bed, in a strange house. I missed Mom and Dad, my annoying little brothers, and the familiar sounds of the nighttime CPR train steaming, puffing and wailing its way through False Creek and out of Vancouver. Those sounds oddly enough were as comforting to this city girl as the intonations of foghorns on winter nights sodden with thick gray mist. If there is such a thing as the yin and yang of country and city life, this was it.

The sun began to climb in the sky promising another day of summer heat and evening mosquitoes while along the rivers edge a train steamed past, heading for the Canyon as we breakfasted on farm-fresh treats before saying our good byes and once again climbing into the station wagon to proceed on our journey.

Entering Clinton, then a town whose main street had wooden sidewalks with railings for tying horses and buildings with a genuine frontier flavor, was exciting and I half expected to see Hopalong Cassidy from the Saturday matinee serials at the Grandview Theatre, riding down from the hillsides. What adventures lay ahead as I learned the tricks of staying on a horse, instead of under it, even when the beast took me beneath the lowest tree branches in an effort to shake me. We visited that wonder of nature, the Painted Chasm, a spectacular and colorful cache in the lava bedrock of the Fraser plateau, and bottomless Emerald Lake from which our fresh-caught trout cooked over an open fire tasted memorably delicious. One evening Cam rowed us out to the center of Loon Lake as dusk fell so we could hear the haunting howls of wolves echoing across the moonlit water as a billion stars winked and glittered from the vast sky above us.

Although we still had to do certain chores and piano practicing, we had fun-filled days capped by evenings with Cam's usually hilarious stories about people with names like the McGillicuddys which for some reason always ensured our childish gales of laughter. Often we took turns making up ghost stories and then when it was time to put out the lights we were too scared to sleep. Although I missed Mom and Dad, I felt secure in the Sutherland's home. They exuded love.

Chapter 35

Apples Of Gold

When school started that September we had our first male teacher. Clayton Williams, fresh out of the navy was short, and freckle faced with reddish-brown curly hair. Amiable, Mr. Williams, as we all called him, was also in charge of the music department. In no time at all he had us singing the lyrical Shenandoah and rowdy What Shall We Do With the Drunken Sailor? We loved him and going to school was a treat.

There was a new boy in our grade five class. To say Gordon was unlike the others would be an understatement. He and his two little sisters had moved with their father into a house a few doors up the street from us. Their mother had recently died and a pleasant housekeeper now cared for them.

His father worked for a large stained glass company and over a period of years would replace most of their home's plain glass windows with his ornately styled stained glass giving the place an eerie, mausoleum feeling. At one point the housekeeper threatened to leave if he installed one more window. Then she married him and he dedicated a new window to her. Seeing her name in glass entwined with swirls and flourishes made all the difference.

The first time Anita, Linda and I went to play at his house we were surprised to find Gordon liked playing dolls. Unlike other boys we knew who had to be threatened with bodily harm before agreeing to even pick up a doll, this new kid adored them, often making his sisters cry when he confiscated their cradles and buggies. He also liked dressing up with us in long gowns, pretty hats, gloves and old high heels.

Gordon seemed unimpressed that his father had a model train setup in their basement that was the envy of every red-blooded boy on our block. The tracks traveled the entire perimeter of their basement, laced with trestles, bridges, a miniature roundhouse, mountains, tunnels and villages for the numerous trains. In fact, the housekeeper once confided to Mom that it was a darned nuisance on laundry day because upon descending the basement stairs with her clothesbasket, she had to first remove sections of track in order to reach the washing machine. The setup was a train buffs dream, but not ten year old Gordon's.

We girls didn't quite know what to do with him. We'd been used to being around boys and brothers who argued, teased, boasted and generally annoyed us. They were all a menace. Now here was blonde-headed, bespectacled Gordon who wanted to be with us.

When Halloween approached Mom planned a party. Aside from my little brothers who had to be included because they lived with us, it would be an all girl party. We'd bob for apples, play games and feast on home made devil's food cake with orange icing. After school that day the basement rec room was decorated with orange and black paper chains and lanterns. No witches, skeletons or black cats for us; ours was a kinder, gentler décor. Cookies and sandwiches wrapped in waxed paper appeared, and the ice box held a new chocolate flavored drink called Topsy, ordered especially that morning from our Crystal Dairy milk man.

Both laundry tubs were filled with cold water and rosy red apples that floated and bobbed tantalizingly on the surface just waiting for us to get our teeth into them.

Six girls and Gordon showed up at party time. His costume was striped overalls, red handkerchief and his father's prized train engineer's cap. Obviously not the costume he'd have chosen, and he looked enviously at the outfits some of us girls were wearing. I was dressed like a Dutch girl, Mom having borrowed a cap from one of her friends who worked at the Window Bakeries in the 1600 block of Commercial Drive where clerks had to be costumed as Dutch girls at all times.

As Gordon tried on my lacey winged Dutch cap, someone tossed his father's cap into our laundry tubs. He screamed and went after it; somehow managing to fall headfirst into the water just as the lights went out. No one ever admitted to pushing him. He had to go home wrapped in Mom's pink chenille bed-jacket while the rest of us fished for his glasses. After that no one wanted to bob for apples because of boy germs. The party came to an abrupt end.

For awhile I sat outside on the wet front steps with Dad who had also had a discouraging evening. It had rained so much his fireworks had fizzled. Grandpa from next door had said it wasn't worth stepping outside for and had disappeared inside for tea and a biscuit with Aunt Til. There was one Roman candle left. Dad positioned it on the drenched lawn; halfheartedly putting lighted punk to wick, which being on the soggy side seemed doomed. The candle spitted and sputtered obstinately before suddenly swooshing up into the night and bursting into droplets of gold before crashing onto the mud. "Wow," said Dad, looking skyward, "it was just like apples of gold!"

Chapter 36

On The Rink Of Disaster

Not too long after we'd gotten used to walking to and from school in autumn sunshine amidst the swirl and crunch of fallen colored leaves underfoot, and the welcoming smell of cinnamon flavored apple pies escaping from Mom's kitchen, to greet our return, than we were into the wet, long days preceding Thanksgiving and Christmas. Mom and Grandma would gather branches of maple leaves at the height of their color, spread them on newspaper and with a paintbrush, give them a coat of varnish to preserve them. When dry, they were placed in vases to provide a bit of fall color until it was time to think about cedar and holly for Christmas decorating.

The Eaton's catalog had arrived and we poured through the pages of insulated parkas, useless to us West Coast kids where rain gear, never included in the eastern based book, was more appropriate. I can't recall Mom ever ordering us anything, but we spent ages leafing through it, snickering at the pages showing long underwear, which Grandpa wore for I'd seen it hanging on his clothesline. There were pictures of uncomfortable looking things called corsets and girdles for women, which I hoped I'd never ever have to wear. This catalog was a far cry from todays

"Wish Book." The only wish book we had was the one in our imagination.

I wanted ice skates. Not just any old ice skates; I wanted white Barbara Ann Scott figure skates. That I'd never even been to an ice rink didn't matter. If only I had the right gear, which would include an outfit and hat trimmed in white fur, I knew I could succeed. I didn't need lessons like my cousin Marilyn who belonged to the elite Vancouver Skating Club.

To my surprise, Dad offered to take me skating at Exhibition Park, on Renfrew and Hastings, the largest rink in Vancouver. He had skated there off and on for years until meeting Mom who didn't skate. After that, his brown leather skates hung by their long laces from a nail in the basement, next to his pin up calendar from the plumbing supplies company, more or less as a melancholy reminder of the good old days. Every once in awhile he'd polish and sharpen the skates, as if readying them for action just in case.

It was a Saturday afternoon when we reached the Hastings Street entrance of the park and descended to the large pit-like basement with dreary fluorescent lighting bouncing off grubby peeling green painted concrete walls. It didn't look inviting at all. Dad rented a pair of skates for me. They were black and rather beat up. We sat on a wooden bench to lace up and I made sure I put my clean pair of extra socks on before slipping my feet into them. Where were the sleek white skates I had envisioned? Dad said those would have to wait. First we'd see how well I could do.

We entered the arena where recorded organ music was playing over loudspeakers and people were skating around and around. The place was gigantic. Wobbling and weaving as I clung to him for dear life, we approached the ice where he tried to skate around holding me up. It wasn't nearly as easy as I'd anticipated and after a few futile efforts I decided to sit on the sidelines while he skated. He was pretty good and I was impressed. I'd never ever pictured my

Dad as a skater. Then it was my turn again. After a series of mishaps and crashes with smart alecs skating too close to us, I was beginning to get cold. My clothes were also wet from the times I'd fallen on the thick white ice. We removed our skates and went downstairs to a concession stand where we each had a hot dog. I was beginning to think this was the best part of my skating debut. Returning to the rink, Dad tried giving me another lesson. I didn't want to do it anymore. What about Barbara Ann Scott and his favorite, Sonja Henie? Wouldn't I like to be like one of them? If you had to be cold and wet, the answer was no. And so we went home. Dad's skates went back on their nail in the basement, Mom made tea and I never again mentioned white skates or the fur outfit.

Chapter 37

Wanted: One Good Housekeeper

The housekeeping situation at Grandpa's was not going well. Aunt Til was about to embark on yet another visit "home" to England. This did not sit well with Harry Cupit. After all, she had already been off to visit her Devonshire relatives twice since he'd hired her to look after him. Aunt Til however, had an independent streak and a nice little war widow's pension.

"You needn't bother coming back," threatened Grandpa as the airport limo picked her up. It wasn't as if he was abandoned for six weeks. Living next door to us, Mom saw to it that he always had plenty of food and a standing invitation with us if he so wished. Besides, he had three other sons and their wives to visit with if he desired. He sat and sulked.

When the six weeks were up and Aunt Til returned he told her she was no longer needed. In a huff, she jammed her felt hat upon her head, bundled herself into the new plaid coat she'd bought in England, packed her belongings, called a taxi and left for her son Mervyns place. This caused a problem in the family for she was Mom's aunt and he was Dad's father. What could be done?

Grandpa went through the Highland Echo ads and hired himself a new housekeeper. Straight from the London blitz *(more or less)* came Mrs. Mac; a plump, brassy cockney who'd undoubtedly suffered through the war years. Her story, told with teary eyes involved the loss of her invalid husband during an air raid when their dwelling was literally sliced in half by a bomb. She had only recently arrived in Canada with her only daughter and son in-law. They were all living in a rooming house on East 3rd Avenue where the handsome, healthy, but mostly unemployed son-in-law spent his days reading the racing forms while his wife worked part time in a hotel laundry.

In record time Mrs. Mac was ensconced in the upstairs back bedroom that had once been Aunt Til's quarters. Things changed rapidly as she went on buying sprees with Grandpa's money. Flowery green and red chintz slipcovers appeared on what had been mostly brown toned furnishings. Colored scatter rugs, flowery drapes and heavily patterned green wallpaper soon followed. I was only a kid, but it looked awful, and didn't go at all with the royal blue velvet curtains that hung between the living room and front hallway to cut the draft. Then a shiny new chrome dinette set with red vinyl upholstered chairs arrived. The wooden kitchen table with its handy cutlery drawer and the familiar wooden chairs vanished... sent to the 3rd Avenue rooming house. It was no longer anything like Grandpa's house. Mom said that Grandma would turn over in her grave if she could see it now.

Mrs. Mac sang music hall songs, danced, told off color stories and smoked! As if that wasn't bad enough, she had tinted reddish blonde hair, wore makeup and dangling earrings. A far cry from my late Grandma who'd never so much as dusted a bit of face powder on her creamy English complexion.

Now, when I went next door to visit Grandpa, Mrs. Mac would be singing, "vote, vote, vote for'arry Cupit, throw old Levie out the door." She'd say to me, "okay luvvy, don't just stand there, give us a tune on the piano!" Cruising Down the River and I've Got a Lovely Bunch of Coconuts were two of her favorites and she belted them out Ethel Merman style. When Grandpa sat reading his Province newspaper and puffing on his pipe, she'd play solitaire at a card table, burning cigarette in the ashtray at hand, occasionally reading a headline aloud as if he hadn't noticed it. He never said anything.

That summer when Auntie Lillian and her family arrived from California for their annual visit, she was apalled and asked Mom and Dad how they'd allowed such a situation to happen? How could her father's house look so garish and how could he eat so much roast beef and Yorkshire pudding topped off by heavy desserts? It was not good for him! Grandpa however, didn't seem to mind his new life-style.

Auntie Lillian thought Mrs. Mac should be given her walking papers and Aunt Til rehired. But it was too late. Aunt Til was now housekeeper for an old widower from Scotland, who had a nice house on Garden Drive, made few demands and had no living relatives. She was not interested in returning to McLean Drive.

Before long, things came to a head. Mrs. Mac's daughter and her lay about husband needed help coming up with their rent money and asked Grandpa to help. When he refused, she suggested they move in to his house. After all, he had two more empty bedrooms. Then a neighbor learned that Mrs. Mac was really not a widow. Indeed her so-called invalid husband killed tragically by a German bomb was alive and well and living with a woman in Wolverhampton.

It was time Uncle Jack, being the eldest son, took matters in hand. He fired Mrs. Mac. Grandpa, now 71 years old never again had a housekeeper. When I dropped in to visit him, usually delivering fresh baked goodies from Mom; he'd be making a meal of bread and cheese. He used the same plate, bowl, cup and cutlery again and again. "Why don't you use different dishes Grandpa?" I'd ask, eyeing the nasturtium patterned china on the open pantry shelves. "Cuts down on the washing up," he'd say. His toaster, covered cheese dish and sugar bowl became permanent fixtures in the center of the chrome and arborite table.

"He's just feeling sorry for himself," Mom would say. "He gets invited out." But he seldom accepted his sons' invitations.

Chapter 38

Shave And A Haircut

On Commercial Drive opposite the shop where Dad worked stood Tommy's Barbershop complete with striped pole at its entrance. Tommy Federici, a smallish energetic white haired man, born in Italy was the owner. His son Jerry, dark-haired with a large moustache worked alongside his Papa in the two-chair establishment.

With three little brothers in our household, a trip to the barber's was a common occurrence, and I'd often be instructed to take one of them to Tommy's for a haircut. It was a job I hated. The place with its checkered linoleum floors was austere. A row of wooden chairs along one wall, a couple of potted palms and spittoons were the only adornment aside from a table of men's magazines all about crime and loose women, upon which I daren't cast my gaze. While electric razors hummed and scissors and combs clicked, I'd sit primly, making a game out of counting the various containers of colored hair tonics lining the glass shelf above the mirrored wall. Bottles of red, green and white Wildroot Cream Oil and Brylcream were interspersed with shaving mugs and brushes. Male friends seemed constantly to be coming in to chat mostly in Italian with Tommy, who amazed me as he slapped hot towels on patrons faces from a steam chest, then lathered and shaved them with a straight razor. As he chattered and laughed, pumping the chair up or down with one foot, and twirling it around, I often wondered how he kept from slicing a customer's throat, for he hardly seemed to be paying attention. Often men would just pass through, disappearing into a back room sequestered behind swinging half doors. What went on out there I never knew, but opera music was always playing in the background. Jerry, probably born in Vancouver, spoke English unless conversing with his father or some of the old-timers. He liked to sing along with the opera stars and did a pretty good Pagliacci. If he were the one cutting my brothers hair, he'd ask about school or my music lessons. But for the most part, I sat silently on a chair dangling my legs, smoothing invisible creases from my dress and wishing the haircut would be over so I could pay the fifty cents and we could leave.

Once outside, we'd take a look in the window of Essen's Bakery a couple of doors down. On Saturdays that was where we'd sometimes buy our bread and once in awhile for a treat, a bag of meringues. Oh how I loved them! Consisting mainly of granulated sugar and egg white, these rosette shaped delicacies were light as air. Dad said they were a waste of money because there was nothing to them.

Mr. Essen, the baker and owner, was a big German who spoke very little English. His only employee was his daughter Effie, a slim pasty complexioned woman with a very plain face not in the slightest enhanced by her blonde hair drawn back in a braided bun. In her white uniform, she seemed almost to have been dipped in one of the flour barrels she was so pale. She seldom smiled. Probably for good reason, for her father constantly barked orders from the back of the shop as she carried the heavy trays of fresh baked goods to the display cases. When she wasn't carefully arranging tarts and cakes on white paper doilies, she was cleaning and polishing the glass showcases. At one time a German flag had hung on the wall, but when the war started, the flag disappeared so that the customers wouldn't. The Essens lived in an apartment directly above the little shop which gleamed and smelled delightful, a far cry from the barber's shop.

Little brother, or brothers in tow, I'd cross the street to see if Dad was in the shop, or out on a job. If he was available, he'd check the haircut. Only once do I remember having to take a brother back to have more off the sides. It was important to get one's 50 cents worth. Before walking home we'd detour over to the lane behind the Crystal Dairy to peek at the Clydesdale horses stabled in back. Until replaced by trucks, these muscular draft horses pulled the wagons on Vancouver's early morning milk deliveries, and although I enjoyed visiting the horses, I secretly hoped a freckle faced boy called Fred would be around. He was in my class at school and I had a crush on him. Because Fred had the dubious honor of living in a house right next to the stables, we all thought he was really lucky.

At the north end of the Drive, just before Williams Street was one of my favorite stores. It was a milliner's shop owned and operated by one of Mom's friends, Jenny, who went to our church. I loved the feeling of her shop. The thickly carpeted place seemed calming. Cream colored cabinets with sliding doors beneath held hat stands displaying feathered, bowed and veiled hats to dream about. A low counter with upholstered velvet chairs held gold-framed swivel mirrors where you could sit and view yourself from different angles as you tried on the various creations. You could have a veil changed, or a ribbon or flower added or subtracted if you so wished. Jenny's workshop was upstairs behind a shuttered balcony, and when you entered the establishment, she'd peek out from her second floor observatory before coming down to assist you. She and her husband lived in quarters behind the store. If she wasn't too busy, she'd make tea for Mom out back. As they chatted, she'd allow me to go upstairs to her workroom and look at the chapeaux in progress. Buckram shapes sat on hat blocks alongside felts and silks. Feathers, ribbon, flowers, fabric and veiling were everywhere as were jeweled ornaments and hand rolled roses. I used to think it would be great living right behind your very own store. I suppose I envisaged being able to get up in the middle of the night just to try on an exotic feather swathed hat. When preferred customers purchased one of Jenny's hats it was wrapped in tissue paper and placed in a round hatbox with carrying handle. As you walked along the Drive, hatbox dangling elegantly from your wrist, everyone knew you had a special date in mind.

Across the street on the east side of Commercial at 1404, was MacIntyre's Men's Wear. When a birthday or Christmas was coming and Mom had to get a gift for one of the men in our family, we would go to see James MacIntyre. The shop glowed from an abundance of polished wood on the walls and counters. Shelves behind the counter seemed almost to touch the ceiling and library style ladders were attached so salesmen could easily reach an item. Boxes held shirts, pajamas, underwear and socks. In the glass fronted counters silk ties, suspenders, cuff links, tie pins, belts, socks, scarves and gloves were displayed. At the back of the store bolts of fabric for men's suits lined the shelves. Harris and Donegal tweeds, herringbones, gabardines, serges and flannels abounded. Everything was a wool or wool blend. Synthetics were unheard of.

Jimmy Robertson, was often wandering about with a tape measure hanging from his neck. Large wooden measuring sticks and tailors chalk sat on the work tables where fabric was measured, smartly snipped with razor sharp shears and pinned to paper patterns ready for basting and fitting. Customers being fitted would stand at the three-way mirror wearing one-sleeved suit jackets as darts and seams were chalked and pinned.

MacIntyre's had been in business on the Drive since 1910 and knew all their customers likes and dislikes so that when I purchased a tie for my Dad all on my own, they were able to whisk out several in tones and patterns of which they knew he'd approve. No bright reds, plaids, or big patterns for him. Subdued blues, grays and the occasional paisley or heather toned mix was more his style. Collar sizes and sleeve lengths for shirts, trouser inseams and hat sizes were all on file for regular customers.

The shops along Commercial Drive met most of our needs. Establishments like Frosts Dry Goods run by a pair of matronly sisters in print dresses was where Mom bought broadcloth to make Dad's pajamas. Bufton's Flowers where the spicy scent of fresh carnations filled the air, was where, once a year on their March wedding anniversary, Dad would purchase a cyclamen plant for Mom. It would always conveniently die before another year rolled around. "You've over-watered it again," Grandma would say, thrusting her finger into the soil.

Wah Lees on the east side corner of Graveley and Commercial sold fresh produce and still tallied up their sales on a Chinese abacus while the old wrinkled grandmother seated out back on a wooden crate, watched from behind the folds of a tattered curtain. Once on a hot summer day when Norm was still my only little brother, we were shopping there with Mom when she fainted. Talking excitedly in Chinese, Wah Lee and his wife carried her out back to revive her with a cup of water. As she disappeared behind the curtain, Norm and I feared she was gone forever. I immediately began to cry, so they gave me some lichee nuts which I didn't know what to do with, having never before seen such things. I stuffed them in Mom's purse. Someone phoned the shop to get Dad to come and pick us all up, but he was out on a job, so his cousin George came to collect us. Mom recovered, but couldn't understand how lichee nuts ended up in her handbag.

Continuing along the east side of the drive, The Sally Shop and Sweet Sixteen were both stores selling moderately priced ladies wear, while Silvers sold more upscale merchandise. The Manitoba hardware, founded in 1905 by Bert Brown liked to boast it'd been in business since nails sold for a penny a pound. At Clapp's Shoes you could stick your feet in their x-ray machine to make certain you were getting a good fit. After Norm, egged on by me, tried to x-ray his head in their device, we never shopped there again. At Woolworth's familiar red and gold fronted 5 and dime store, Anita and I would eventually get our first after school jobs. Further down the drive, Hallett's Café with a soda fountain was where on rare occasions Dad would take a brief coffee break. Their booths were fitted with machines in which you inserted a coin and your favorite selection would play on their jukebox.

We didn't often go downtown, but if we did The Bay was Dad's preference. While Mom pondered over bolts of fabric in the dry goods department, Dad would take us to the malt bar at the bottom of the first floor escalator. Thick and creamy chocolate malts served in a small paper cup with a wooden spoon for scooping were a real treat. No seating was provided. You just propped yourself and any packages against a pillar, and for entertainment, watched shoppers feverishly pawing through the bargain basement wares. This was where Uncle Jack liked to do his shopping, although his wife, Auntie Marion preferred the more upscale Chapman's. Dad always said bargain basement stores smelled funny, like old rubber tires and onions, so once we'd eaten our treat we retreated to the Bay's main floor to wait for Mom.

There weren't many places to get a quick meal in downtown Vancouver at that period. Woolworth's on Granville Street just down from The Bay had a lunch counter, but when we felt hungry we headed home for soup and a sandwich.

Chapter 39

The Circus Comes To 1416

A couple of times a year our living room at 1416 became center stage for an honest to goodness circus performer, Barney the sword swallower.

He was retired; a widower who with his late wife had traveled the carnival circuit year in and year out weaving through numerous dusty little backwoods communities that ultimately blended. It had been a hard life with little glory aside from the magic that happens when an entertainer experiences that wonderful aphrodisiac known as applause.

But now, Barney Barnetto lived alone in a couple of rooms papered in faded circus posters in the back of a moldering building behind the plumbing and sheet metal shop where Dad worked. As he labored, Barney would often appear at the open back doorway to regale him with circus stories. Feeling sorry for the lonely old fellow, Dad would sometimes feel obliged to extend a dinner invitation.

Mom would make extra meat loaf, accompanying vegetables and fresh apple pie for dessert and a deal would be struck. Toothless

Barney would work for his meal. Not that he was expected to... he just liked the idea of doing a performance.

After dinner he'd set up the kitchen chairs in our living room, then hand me a dingy, tattered piece of sheet music entitled Beautiful Lady in Blue. I was to be his accompanist on the piano. My little brothers eagerly took their places with Dad while Mom rather gingerly handed Barney the accoutrements necessary for his act and substituting for swords... kitchen knives! The bigger and sharper the better. Looking at them, we'd cringe in anticipation. But first he'd pile a couple of wooden chairs atop one another, crowned by our high-legged kitchen stool. Then, tension mounting, he'd go off stage, *(so to speak)*, our front hall becoming the wings, give me a nod and I'd begin pounding the piano keys to his signature melody.

Barney would make his entrance and begin pulling multicolored scarves from his sleeves and doing various magic tricks to the delight and applause of my brothers. Then he'd climb the "tower" so we could see him better, and perching himself with head held back would proceed to somehow make our ordinary old knives disappear down his throat right to their hilts. Ouch!

That he had no teeth, and talked with a funny hoarse voice only made us wonder uneasily if he had become a sword swallower in spite of, or because of a mishap. We never knew. Then, show time over, he'd beckon me to take a bow while he clapped and thanked me! I felt like a star, even if he was a funny old has-been.

Dad would help him on with his tatty old raincoat with its missing buttons and threadbare lining while Mom pressed a box of her home baking into his large hands. Then, faded copy of Beautiful Lady folded and squeezed under his arm, he'd depart. While Dad drove him home, we kids got ready for bed and Mom boiled our cutlery.

Chapter 40

My Daughter's No Shill

Barney wasn't the only character in our lives who was in show business. Although at an altogether different end of the spectrum, Wesley Stewart, a street corner evangelist, was also a performer. How he became an acquaintance of our family I've no idea, for although regular churchgoers, we were not given to outward displays of zeal or God forgive, proselytizing, especially in public.

Dad's cousins on his mother's side were Baptists. Like some of the other mainstream religions there are different degrees of Baptists. In fact, Dad's cousin's cousin, Harold, started his very own church near the Grandview Cut, and became a preacher after having fallen out with mainline Baptist beliefs. When things were quiet in the religion end of things, or when it took more than faith to put bread on the table for his large family, he worked at the plumbing and sheet metal shop run by his and Dad's cousin, George.

Wesley it seems was one of those freethinking revivalists of the hell fire and brimstone variety. He would show up every once in awhile to hang about the shop. Perhaps he'd be visiting Harold and George and then get to talking to Dad who was never much of a conversationalist, but would feign interest by intermittently saying um hum which was all the encouragement a person like Wesley needed. Because Dad was not of the Baptist faith he probably felt a need to redeem his soul. It didn't matter that Dad was our church treasurer and chairman of the board.

A well-leafed soft covered edition of the King James Bible was always in Wesley's possession. With its soiled pages and red marked passages the dog-eared word of the Lord was testimony in itself. He liked to gather a group about him on the roughest corners of downtown Vancouver; places like Main and Hastings outside the Carnegie Library. But he could turn up on unlikely corners like Broadway and Commercial or Granville and Georgia outside of the Bay, until encouraged to move along by the local constable walking his beat. And although he dressed in a suit and tie and kept his thick white hair neatly trimmed, once launched into his preaching he was much like a worked up John the Baptist crying in the wilderness while insisting everyone repent before it was too late. Once when he refused to quit preaching, they loaded him into the paddy wagon, and as they drove away, he yelled through the bars at the top of his voice, "you brood of vipers!"

Mom had no use for Wesley. Indeed, if we ever encountered him on the Drive as we were shopping, I had been advised to ignore him and walk fast. This I did with little hesitation. And so when he actually showed up at our front door one day, let in by one of my well-meaning little brothers who led him into the kitchen, Mom was, to put it lightly, upset! What did he want?

As I came up the back steps from school I heard her berating him, "I'm not about to have my daughter used as some kind of shill, now get out of here!" Hat and bible in hand, he left the house as Mom, seething went to the telephone to relate the story to anyone and everyone she knew beginning with Grandma. I stood there wondering what on earth a shill was? Seems Wesley had seen me with Dad and thought he could get a few more converts on the street corners if I accompanied him. He'd mentioned the possibility to Dad who not paying attention to the conversation answered with um hum, just to shut him up. Taking that as a possible yes, Wesley had walked on down to our house to suggest the idea to Mom who was not impressed. For ages after that, whenever Wesley's name came up Mom would start in with, "the nerve of that creature, thinking I'd let my daughter drum up business for him!"

Chapter 41

There's Silver In Those Teeth

When I sat in Dr. Crowhurst's chair at the Medical Dental Building at 925 West Georgia Street, I didn't appreciate the fact I was sitting in one of Vancouver's most elegant art nouveau treasures. Nor did I care much that as a bricklayer, Grandpa had helped build the structure.

Little did I realize as we entered through brass and glass polished doors of the chevron-clad skyscraper to the cooling marble interior, that this hallowed structure would one day *(1989)* be demolished; a thing of beauty forever lost to our city. None of that crossed my mind as Dad and I went up, up, up in the elevator with uniformed attendant calling out the floors and sliding open the two sets of doors. Indeed as I sat there being tortured with drills, picks, needles, suction hoses, rubber dams and a dour-faced nurse telling me when to spit, art nouveau was not on my mind. Novocaine was!

I spent many unhappy Saturday mornings each year in that dentist's office, it's only redeeming feature being the view from the window of Burrard Inlet, the North Shore mountains, or Coal Harbor and Stanley Park. Once in awhile a jet-lagged sea gull would perch on the ledge and I'd wish I were free to fly away when he did.

Despite the fact I brushed and flossed diligently, whenever Dad took me for my yearly checkup, I needed some fillings.

The austere waiting room was tiny, white, crisp and clinical not unlike Miss Henry, the unsmiling nurse. A far cry from today's dental establishments with their individual television sets, or music tailored to the patient's likes, Dr. Crowhurst's office boasted no such accoutrements. Feeling like a victim, I sat in the hard black leatherette chair next to a constantly gurgling white sink, trying not to count the vast collection of instruments on the porcelain platelike table. Ever the child with a wild imagination, I wondered fearfully what that tiny flame encased in chrome was going to be used for? But I couldn't ask because there was a piece of rubber sheeting jammed in my mouth so I wouldn't choke on bits of flying enamel once the drilling began. I hated the sound of that drill as much as I hated having a frozen mouth.

In an effort to bribe me to go to the dentist peacefully, for I had once kicked Dr. Crowhurst in the shins, Dad always took me up the street to my store of dreams after the torture. Birks Jewelers at Georgia and Granville would be doomed for demolition in 1974. In the 1940's however, thoughts of it ever being the victim of a wrecker's ball were as unthinkable as not being able to rendezvous on that very corner beneath their famous clock.

Birks had a hushed quality about it, maybe because the presence and sound of the cash registers ring was absent. When a purchase was made the invoice and money was placed in a tube and sent who knows where? Dad said it went upstairs to an office. I envisioned someone up there like Scrooge McDuck rolling about in mounds of gold and silver.

I managed to acquire several small pieces of silver jewelry in accordance to the amount of pain I felt I'd endured down the street at the Medical Dental. With a frozen mouth it was often difficult to make my wants known, so I'd just point at a particular bauble in the accepted price range. Just when I was well on the way to having a silver bracelet laden with charms and a collection of their small blue boxes, with which to play jewelers, I had a checkup in which Dr. Crowhurst announced, "no new cavities!" Then, trying a little humor he added, "you must have been eating your carrot sticks!" Dad was so happy he took me to Birks... and, had his wristwatch cleaned!

Chapter 42

Pining For The Bogs

The Sunday before Christmas we would travel out to Lulu Island to get a tree because the area abounded with pines, a favorite of Dad's. We were not responsible for the clear cutting that eventually took place in the area, which had been named incongruously after a San Francisco showgirl called Lulu Sweet.

Driving to Lulu Island was an all-afternoon excursion in pre-freeway times and excitement mounted as we neared our favorite knoll. No sooner had our Chevrolet rolled to a stop than my three little brothers would be all over the terrain like jays at a sunflower feeder. "Here's one Daddy, this one's perfect, come on let's get this one, it's even better," their voices escalating with excitement as they darted from grove to grove.

By this time I was a little more sophisticated and stuck close to Dad as he calmly looked over tree after tree, rejecting each for one reason or another. Much like the story of Goldilocks and the three bears, one was too small, one too big, one too sparse. I pointed out another, which Mom loved, but shaking his head, Dad proclaimed it too bushy for our living room. He knew which one he wanted and we weren't likely to sway his decision.

It was about 4:30 p.m. and the December fog had rolled in making tree appraisal more difficult. Mom had gone back to sit in the car because she was getting cold and the choice of a tree, like most of Dad's decisions, was taking a long time. Being the only girl on site, and as my brothers slugged it out amongst themselves, having long ago lost interest in tree hunting, I decided to use my powers of persuasion. Indeed, I felt it my duty, and immediately pointed out a pine upon which Dad smiled approval. He headed in the direction of the glossy enchantress, its numerous healthy looking candles and firm brown cones taunting.

Dad had only a couple more steps to be in reach of this prize specimen when PHEWSH, without warning, he suddenly sunk to belt level in the boggy mess, axe now wielded high overhead, still wearing with proud bearing, his natty tweed hat and Sunday suit.

After we'd hauled him out, giggling nervously, he refused to get our tree, and for the entire ride home to Grandview, we kids intermittently pouted because we were treeless, or snickered because poor Daddy's uncomfortable mud-impregnated clothing squished every time he moved.

That was the first Christmas we installed a tree purchased from a Commercial Drive gas station lot in our living room. It wasn't a pine! Mom said he'd gone off pines for this year. Dad still made the wooden stand for the tree, but the old magic was gone.

Chapter 43

Grandpa's Politics

Most Friday evenings I still visited next door for a couple of hours with Grandpa where we'd discuss the events of the week. This meant he'd go through the Province and tell me how ridiculous everybody was. Mayor Fred Hume who lived high atop West Vancouver's Sentinel Hill ruled Vancouver and raised Grandpa's dander. Every Christmas he'd light his aerie for all to see from the Vancouver side. Despite the fact he owned western Canada's largest electrical contracting company, Hume and Rumble, and as a philanthropist was donating his Mayor's salary to charity, Grandpa thought it a disgusting display of wealth. I thought it looked pretty.

Vancouver residences and businesses were rarely outlined in lights. Christmas trees and tinsel abounded in nearly every window, but that was the extent of holiday décor. Neon lights shone forth on main streets like Granville's theatre district, but there were few illuminated Christmas displays.

After I'd listened to Grandpa's opinionated reviews I'd play the piano for him, always beginning with his favorite, My Bonnie Lies Over the Ocean which he'd sing, eyes tear-filled by the time we got to the last line, Oh bring back my Bonnie to me. He'd wipe his eyes with his handkerchief as I pretended not to notice. Then we'd sing I'll take you home again Kathleen and Just a Song at Twilight. We often ended with Oh Little Town of Bethlehem, even when it wasn't Christmas because that had been Grandma's favorite.

Returning home with the five dollars spending money he always gave me, I'd sit on the wooden kitchen stool and tell Mom everything Grandpa had told me and she'd say, "don't pay any attention to him or his silly politics." But what were his politics? I knew he argued sometimes for more than an hour on the street corner with Mrs. Roth, the Liberal from down the street. And I knew she'd angrily denounced him as a Socialist. But I also knew his entire family were Conservatives. Did he insist on going on about all politicians just being out to line their pockets, to antagonize people and get into a good argument? I think so, for I knew how he delighted in egging people on, for he often did that with Mom. She'd say to Dad, "I know he's your father, but I'm never speaking to him again!" It would last for a few days and then she'd relent and invite him for supper. He was a tyrant and with a sly smile would say to her, "well my dear, did you finally see the error of your ways?" Then it would be round two.

Chapter 44

Raincoats And Snuggies

Now that I was attending Templeton Junior High, on the corner of Templeton Drive and Adanac Street, bounded on the north by Turner Street and Lakewood Drive on the west, I had a long walk to and from school. Anita and I had to leave by 8 a.m. She would call on me as I was usually running late, hating to get up, particularly on winter mornings.

Mom would yell at the foot of the stairs, "Joan, get up! Your porridge is going cold." And by the time I got to it, it was. Then looseleaves, textbooks and lunch bags in our arms we'd begin the walk. We first trudged up the three steep city blocks on Graveley to Commercial, then to Grant Street, up Grant to Salisbury Drive where we continued along passing Kitchener, Charles, William and Napier Streets to Parker, and then on to Victoria, Semlin and Lakewood Drives to Templeton Drive. Sometimes we varied our route, but a city block was a city block and there were no shortcuts.

Temp, as we called it, was for grades 7 to 9 and with its three floors of hallway monitored classrooms; cafeteria, gymnasium, auditorium and playing field seemed gigantic to us after having attended such a small elementary school. Aside from the kids with whom I'd shared six years at Woodland Elementary, I only knew two other students... my third cousins Stanley and Ronnie. I had been warned by my grandmother to stay away from them, so immediately looked them up. They were both in grade 9, and compared to me, terribly worldly. They hung out with a gang and when the bell rang, Stan in particular took his own sweet time sauntering to class. He chewed gum, spit, smoked and sometimes swore. I was absolutely shocked. After all, I had only mixed with him and Ronnie when they were visiting my Grandma or I was visiting theirs; occasions when they'd be on their best behavior. Because our grandma's were sisters, one living on Parker Street and the other on Venables, not many secrets were kept.

Although he would go on to teach at John Oliver in a year, at that time Uncle Frank taught French at Temp, and his good friend and neighbor Jimmy Grant was principal. Frank Calder in the Science department was also an old family friend, along with Bert Libbey, school counselor. I knew all these people and their wives socially through visits with them at Uncle Frank and Auntie Marg's or at Uncle Ernie and Auntie Elsie's.

I was a plodding C+ student, a daydreamer who filled empty loose-leaf pages with sketches and scribblings instead of paying attention. Now here I was in a school where one of my most favorite uncles and his colleagues would soon discover what a dummy I really was. Science taught by Mr. Calder and Math taught by Mr. Frost who was the brother of Walter, our church treasurer, were my worst subjects and my first report card showed C minuses. I was a failure. In an effort to cover up scholastic inadequacies, I began my career as class comic. It was easy and made the kids and sometimes the teachers laugh.

Anita was getting A's and B's as usual, and although we now had few classes together she tried to get me to smarten up. Dad tried helping me with math and science, which when done by him always had the correct answers although arrived upon by different methods.

On one report card I managed to bring my Science up to a B, but was doomed to carry on in the C minuses at best in math and physical ed. How anybody could fail gym class astounded members of the athletic Cupit family.

Forced to join the girls grass hockey team, I found myself practicing on the field with a bunch of aggressive females who believed in winning. They weren't interested in playing just for fun like our old ball team on McLean Drive had done. Venables Street where Grandma and Uncle lived was just a block from Templeton, and Uncle who was a big soccer and cricket fan, would often stop to watch us enroute to a Hastings Street bakery for a loaf of fresh homestyle bread.

Little did I realize he often stood on the sidelines getting a good laugh out of my efforts to hit the ball, and at the legs of my pale pink cotton snuggies that kept falling down below my navy blue gym shorts. In fall and winter, because of the long walk, Mom insisted I wear the stupid things to keep my thighs warm. No matter how I rolled the legs up, they always drooped during the game. I spent more time rolling and tucking than engaging the ball. It was a miserable experience until I got hold of a pair of scissors.

Having solved the snuggies problem I realized there was a dress code of sorts. If you weren't in the right clothes you didn't count. Navy blue trench coats were in and I didn't have one. Purple Seagrams bags with gold cords were popular for purses too, but I came from a non-drinking household. It seemed really important to me that I have a coat like everyone else although Mom and Grandma tried to convince me it was better to be different.

I've no idea how much trench coats cost in the 1950's, but it was obvious the purchase of one was not in our budget. And then one day, arriving home from school, I was greeted with a surprise... a trench coat! It wasn't new; Elsie Kay's Auntie Margaret had given it to me. I could hardly wait to open the brown paper package. And there it was... a lime green trench coat! Much as I tried to explain it had to be navy blue, I got nowhere. The next day I set off for Temp wearing the hated coat. Stanley and Ronnie howled with laughter, and Stan suggested throwing the coat away and telling Mom it got stolen, but how was I going to walk home coatless in the cold? Sanity prevailed, and as much as I detested the coat, I wore it. Then one rainy afternoon when walking through Victoria Park, alone because Anita was home sick, I heard a whistle from the far side of the park. It was a wolf whistle followed by the loud voice of freckle-faced Fred, the boy from the house adjoining the Crystal Dairy Stables. "Who's the slick chick in the pea-green rain coat?" Suddenly the coat didn't seem all that bad.

Chapter 45

See How We Grovel

Auntie Muriel who was in the Eastern Star decided I should be doing something worthwhile and mixing with "better" people. She decided to pay for me to join Job's Daughters. Meetings were held weekly at Bethel Number One, on 1st Avenue just above Commercial Drive. After initiation, the idea was to work hard and go through the chairs until you became a princess and finally honored queen. There was a secret handshake and password. At the conclusion of every meeting, as the lights were dimmed and a spotlight shone on the queen and princesses, a girl who happened to be the scandalous daughter of an Anglican priest, sang "Come holy Spirit, heavenly dove." As she reached the part about, "look how we grovel here below, fond of these earthly toys," I substituted the word "boys" and broke everyone up. This was not a good thing.

I disliked Jobs Daughters for several reasons; the main one being the fact Anita could never become a member because she was Roman Catholic. It didn't seem right. And why should I have to call some girl in a cheap white satin gown and purple robe, honored queen? What did I care about being one of the fairest in the land? The Masonic Order was not for this free thinker. Before long, and much to Auntie Muriel's displeasure, I was kicked out.

Despite my failure as a gifted student or a Job's Daughter, I still loved my music lessons. Every Thursday after school, zippered black music case in hand, I headed for Nancy Borthwick's house on Kitchener Street just opposite Victoria Park, then a rather pleasant square of green lawns ringed with Canadian maple and English oak trees. For an hour she would try to encourage me to play the music exactly the way it was written by the composer. I preferred variations.

Nancy was a patient, kind and quiet gray-haired lady who sang in the soprano section of our choir. Unmarried, she had for many years looked after her elderly father, a professor of music who until his death had been organist at Grandview United. She now lived alone in the cold old house where she taught piano and voice lessons in the front parlor warmed in winter by one little heater. It was a cheerless place with frayed carpets, worn furniture and stacks of old music everywhere. Crippled from birth, Nancy sometimes wore an ugly elevated black shoe on one foot, which seemed only to draw attention to her infirmity.

At some point there was really no more she could teach me on the piano, so I then studied voice with her. Vienna My City of Dreams and various sacred solos followed. Because Anita and I went to every Hollywood musical that graced the screen of the Grandview Theatre, I longed to sing show tunes and often spent my weekly allowance on popular sheet music. Now, besides listening to my daily piano practice the family had to put up with my attempts at singing. While Mom wrestled with preparing dinner for the six of us and keeping my little brother's at bay, I sat singing at the piano, fancying myself as the next Doris Day or Jane Powell.

Poor Dad would come home from a hard days work seeking peace and quiet, not me belting out, "You sure have been a liar, you know you've been a liar, all your good for nothin' life," from Royal Wedding. But he never said anything, at least to me.

Sometimes in an effort to get me away from the piano, Mom would insist I help with dinner. I'd set the table and do a flower arrangement, which went unnoticed in a cramped kitchen full of noisy, hungry males to whom stew and dumplings meant more than any tastefully executed bouquet of pansies and parsley.

Chapter 46

Lunches At Grandma's

Although I sometimes wanted to be "one of the gang" and fit in with the kids at Temp, another part of me, my more timid side won out, and instead of joining in with the noisy cafeteria crowd I chose to walk one block up the street to the comfort of Grandma's kitchen on Venables.

I'm sure Mom and Dad paid her a bit of money towards my lunches and wonder now if she really relished being tied down by her 12 year old granddaughter five noon hours a week. However, since she always had Uncle to consider except on library day when he took the streetcar to the Carnegie for his books, she may not have minded.

The buzzer would sound at 12 o'clock and by ten past I'd be at Grandma's front door. Having run up the stone garden steps, then the numerous front steps leading to her immaculately maintained gray front porch with the brown wicker furniture, I'd twist the metal door bell ringer of the heavy front door, it's oval glass shielded for privacy by sheers.

Once inside, I'd wash up in the downstairs bathroom before taking my place at the kitchen table with it's high backed cream painted wooden chairs. An old hutch set on a sideboard was also painted cream and held a display of English china plates decorated with red windblown poppies, a biscuiteer with a silver lid, and a beige and green humidor. A black and white portrait of me as a barefooted, towheaded toddler seated on a twig garden bench hung on the wall above the hutch, as did a picture of Grandpa Phillifant taken the summer before his death.

Grandma and Uncle took their places at the big square table and we bowed our heads and said grace. At our house we only said grace on Sundays, but Grandma said we should be thankful every day. Usually lunch consisted of eggs and bacon or homemade soup and bread. It was here that I first tasted ox-tail, and mulligatawny, two soups that would never appear in our bowls on Graveley Street. At Grandma's I learned to enjoy caraway seed buns, almond tarts, stollen, English Stilton, and ginger beer, a non-alcoholic drink that made your throat burn and your eyes water. From Grandma I learned to love biscuits or fresh bread spread with homemade raspberry jelly and topped with Devonshire Clotted Cream. Despite the fact Dad had been born in England, he considered all this English food served by his mother-in-law to be foreign. When I said I liked it, Mom said, "just wait 'til Grandma serves you tripe and onions!" She never did.

On Fridays, because that was the day Grandma washed and waxed all the floors and polished everything within an inch of its life, in readiness for the weekend, we had simple salmon sandwiches. That day we had to be careful to walk on sections of newspaper leading like a pathway from the front hallway through to the kitchen and pantry so we wouldn't mark up her clean linoleum. In the kitchen two big windows looked down upon second cousin Jack and Millie's bungalow, the twin to our Graveley Street house, for Grandpa had helped build both. Starched lace curtains on these windows helped conceal the comings and goings of Stanley, their errant teenaged son.

An electric range was the only appliance in Grandma's kitchen. Hidden behind a weighted swinging butler's door; the pantry contained cupboards, the marble counters that had been salvaged by Grandpa from the walls of a demolished 18th century hotel washroom, and the kitchen sink where Uncle generally washed the dishes. Grandma didn't own a refrigerator so things like butter, milk, and creamo were kept in a basement icebox. If you fancied an ice cream cone, you walked a block to the little corner store on Venables and Lakewood. At the close of that school year, I missed having lunches with Grandma and Uncle, but still saw them most Sundays after church when we all gathered around the dining room table for family dinner.

Chapter 47

Why Tacoma?

Our August vacation that year was a short car trip to Washington state where we followed the Chuckanut route in Bellingham, probably bringing back pleasant memories to Dad and Mom who had driven that trail in 1936 on their honeymoon. Now, twelve years hence, there were six of us.

After Everett and Seattle things were going so well Mom and I urged Dad to drive on to Oregon and maybe California where we would visit the McLarnin's. But, on the outskirts of Tacoma, after running over a skunk which visited its' revenge upon us by bending one of the cars' rims and permeating our vehicle and contents with a pungent odor, we found ourselves limping into the nearest gas station. The old proprietor asked us to please park away from the pumps because we smelled so bad he felt it would drive patrons away. As motorists pulled up to one or other of the two round pumps with glass Shell insignias on top; they'd ask what the awful stink was before quickly rolling up any open windows. The guy would point in our direction and say, "Skunk." How embarrassing. To obtain a new tire and rim for our '39 Chevrolet, a bit of time would be needed. It was now late afternoon.

As luck would have it, an auto court adjoined the gas station. We found ourselves spending two nights in a unit called Bide-A-Wee, unknown to tourists then or now as a paradise destination. But the kindly owners doused our car tires with tomato juice to help rid us of the skunk stigma and put us in their largest unit where the most exciting feature was a four-slot toaster that the slices of bread actually walked through. We ate a lot of toast.

When our car was once again ready for the road, Dad wasn't in any mood to go further south. The expense of a new rim and tire hadn't cheered him. Following a very short shopping trip in Tacoma where I tried unsuccessfully to get them to buy me a new rain coat so the lime green one could be passed on to another fledgling, we headed north for home. I don't recall sulking for too long though because I had a new gray corduroy jacket and saddle shoes.

Chapter 48

From Skunks To Storks

Summer holidays were coming to an end as the majority of Vancouver kids looked forward to the annual PNE parade heralding the opening of the Pacific National Exhibition. It was always a huge parade with beautiful floats, marching bands, clowns and acrobats. The route began downtown and covered all of Hastings Street until reaching the PNE grounds at Renfrew Street. There, numerous exhibits, food galore and Happy Land with the Ferris wheel, big and small dipper, shoot the chute and various other exciting rides awaited.

This year our family would find itself much involved in the PNE parade because Mom had taken on an awesome project, and it was about to happen in our back yard.

Garson Kanin's hit play Born Yesterday was rehearsing for production at North Vancouver's Totem Theatre, an outdoor summer stock venue that sadly would only last a few seasons. Uncle Les, working for a large advertising agency, was promoting the play of Judy Holiday fame and a star from New York was to be in the lead. This was considered really big time and when Les mentioned to Mom that they wanted to put a float in the parade to gain publicity and would she be interested, she offered to fix something up. She was like that. Artistic juices ran through her veins and in no time she'd designed something.

Arrangements made, a couple of slick looking types who happened to be Arngrim and Baker, the theatre's owners and producers, pulled up our back lane in a canary yellow Buick convertible. The vehicle was to be decked out with Mom's creation... a giant stork, pre Big Bird style, holding a sling in its mouth which would transport the star of the show who'd be wearing nothing but a shimmering gold bathing suit and mink stole. Pretty daring!

Our typical east Vancouver yard was about 30 feet wide with Dad's decrepit double garage standing guard at the back of it. There was no driveway or off property parking area. Problem number one arose. The Buick couldn't be decorated inside the garage because the floorboards couldn't take the added weight. Nor would there be enough room height wise by the time a stork was added. But the car wouldn't fit in our yard either, unless part of the fence was removed and some of the vegetable garden encompassed by the gooseberry patch that provided annually for Dad's favorite pies was expropriated. The sacrifice made, Mom began crafting hundreds of white crepe paper feathers to plump out the papier mache over wire frame of the stork which upon completion would be anchored securely in place atop the generous sized, chrome laden Buick.

Remembering how she immersed herself in projects, I'm sure she hated having to stop and prepare meals for Dad and us four kids, but she did it. There were no microwaves, fast food, or pizza deliveries to fall back on.

As the stork took on life, nearby residents gathered to hang over rose-tumbled fences and watch the proceedings while Grandpa from next door, surveyed the production with amusement, drawing on his ever-present pipe and shaking his head in disbelief.

The eyes of the stork were an engineering feat; huge soulful looking things with long curly lashes that could flutter open and shut via a cable connected to a cigarette holder to be held by the actress riding in the sling.

Finally all was in readiness. The stork was finished and with Dad's help placed firmly in position in the convertible's back seat where it towered in all its glory. Neighbors and friends came by and applauded Mom. She was a celebrity, at least until the star of Born Yesterday came by to try out her perch, causing excited bystanders bearing box Brownie cameras to begin clicking shutters through hedges.

That night, the eve of the parade, not surprisingly, it rained. The first pitter pats danced upon our roof about 9 p.m. and were met with great activity from all within. We had to run outside and try to cover the grinning stork along with the convertible, which was now in danger of becoming an expensive wading pool. Since this was the era before all night shopping and the convenience of being able to rush out and buy great rolls of plastic drop sheets, we had to improvise. Bird and car were enveloped in a canopy of raincoats, a tarp, shower curtain, and anything else remotely waterproof.

The rain decreased to an intermittent West Coast drizzle as the night wore on, and at dawn the sun shone as the wraps were removed and a driver arrived to take the car to the parades starting point. Mom prepared our breakfast and as Dad left for work we kids eagerly dressed and readied ourselves for the walk to Hastings Street to find a viewing place on the route. We walked, block after block after block. It was a long way and the morning was warming up. I began lagging behind as Mom urged, "come on, or we'll miss it!" My three little brothers, known collectively as "the boys," skipped, jumped and ran in and out around telephone poles, excitement mounting. Twenty blocks and many minutes later we were there curbside as the stork glided by, eyes fluttering, actress blowing kisses and a fellow walking alongside the car admonishing everyone to get tickets for Born Yesterday. Dad had managed to get a few minutes off work to catch a glimpse of the stork going by on Heatley Avenue. In his quiet way he was proud of her and at supper that night told us, "Mom can do anything!" I think we always believed it.

A photo made it into one of the daily papers and for a time the stork was used as a theatre lobby's prop. Back home at 1416, the fence pickets went in place once again and life continued. But for some reason, the somewhat trampled gooseberry bushes produced the most yummy pies on record that summer.

Chapter 49

Sayonara

Our neighborhood was changing even more as the fifties unfolded. Despite the fact Grandview had long been home to some mix of Italian, Chinese and eastern Europeans, until now it had remained predominantly WASP territory. "Home" to most of our neighbors had been England. Now, however, a second larger wave of immigrants descended upon us. Our street began to change noticeably as many of the old-timers moved on to newer neighborhoods in other parts of Vancouver.

Instead of hearing all about what was going on in England, now when the neighbors talked over the picket fences which once had protected typically English cutting gardens, the chatter was in other languages. Where once the smell of roast beef and Yorkshire pudding had filled the air, garlic fortified dishes wafted on the wing. Conversations that had once been about the cricket match were now about boccie.

Grandpa didn't like it one bit. "By Jove, these people can't even speak English," he announced from behind his Vancouver Daily Province. "How are they going to vote properly?" In fact, Japanese-Canadians had just recently won the right to vote at all.

It wasn't just our street that changed. As the fifties progressed, there were many differences in the faces around Britannia, the small high school of a few hundred students, that I attended. Because all my aunts and uncles had graduated from Brit, I was expected to do the same. It was the academic school. If you weren't planning on going to university, you went to Vancouver Technical School out on Broadway where you could learn a trade or take classes in commerce.

Because Anita enrolled at Tech, I began my high school years minus the best friend I'd shared just about everything with since elementary days. I didn't relish the idea of attending Brit; in fact once again I didn't really want to go to school. To sit in my room where I could write, sketch, and read Nancy Drew mysteries or movie magazines would have suited me fine. Glossy photos of Robert Wagner and Rock Hudson now hung on my bedroom wall. I'd sent away to Hollywood for them and dreamed of being swept off my feet by one or other of them, or failing that, a home grown look alike. Lance, a boy from our church who lived just down the street from Grandma's, looked like he could be a Robert Wagner one day. But he always punched me on the arm and called me Mouse. Not terribly sophisticated.

Grandpa said I should carry on the family tradition and become a schoolteacher. To him, a teaching degree was the highest attainment. We already had several teachers in our family. I didn't think we needed to sacrifice anymore. It didn't matter that I had other ideas or that Mom was eagerly suggesting I become a dress designer or concert pianist. Dad was just too busy earning a living for all of us to inject any ideas he might have had for me. I think he just hoped for an epiphany. Suddenly, I'd see the light and be able to do Math homework without his help!

By 1953 Britannia, still considered a small city school of about 350 students, had become predominantly Oriental in makeup. A large percent of the kids in my classes were now either newly arrived

or second generation born in Vancouver Japanese or Chinese. Although I had caucasian friends, they lived in areas up above Nanaimo and Hastings. After school they headed home to Hastings east while I strolled along Woodland Drive in the opposite direction. Now my Grandview friends encompassed girls with names like Shikitani and Ono. They had a lot of the same interests as me; art, music and poetry. They were also good at algebra and geometry, subjects still giving me problems. When I stooped to the level of having a newly arrived Chinese boy who spoke no English, feed me the correct answers, I knew I was in trouble. My math teacher annoyed Mom by saying that since I was pretty, maybe I'd get married young and wouldn't need math.

Unlike a lot of kids, who hung around Commercial Drive cafes drinking coffee and smoking after school, these new friends had little time for such things because they also attended Japanese School. They were excellent students, treated their teachers with respect, and seemed driven to succeed. The only thing driving me was the urge to perfect my one-liners and keep the class laughing. And then I met Miss Mayse.

She taught English class and stories of her strictness preceded our introduction. With her short clipped grey hair, favored plain brown tweed suits and sensible oxfords, she didn't look like a person who would appreciate my humor. And she didn't, unless I showed it in a composition. Lenny the Litter-lout, a piece about a boy with a piggy locker was given an A and hung on the wall. Others followed. I decided perhaps one could get by in life without being a math whiz. Grandpa disagreed.

"How are you going to balance your cheque book or play chess?" I explained I knew how to add and subtract, and I didn't care about playing chess. Mom said, "don't worry about him, he was a bricklayer! What do bricklayers know about math?" I noticed Dad looked at her kind of funny when she said that, but he remained quiet.

As I became better acquainted with the Japanese families in our neighborhood, I sometimes went to their homes. Most were of the Christian faith, but one family was Shintoist. When I went to their house with its fierce looking idols sequestered inside tokonomas it seemed very strange indeed. As a matter of fact, it wasn't until their fisherman father heard who my father was and that he was an honorable man respected in the community, that they finally allowed me inside. This had never happened before. What was going on?

One day I was treated to a fashion show as the girls modelled beautiful silk kimonos and obis, which they would wear for a festival. To be clothed in the traditional costume and all it's accessories, they stood upon chairs to be wound, draped and tucked. Standing in their white stockinged feet, whining impatiently for a cold coke, they made remarks in English so their Japanese speaking mothers couldn't understand them. The delicate hair ornaments that dangled almost like tiny wind chimes were the final touch and absolutely charmed me. I remember returning home along Woodland Drive that spring afternoon, passing beneath the falling, fluttering petals of Mrs. Marcasey's magnolia tree, wishing I had some fascinating heritage other than English so I could dress up and go to an exotic festival.

The closest thing we had to sustain our ancestry was the St. George's Day Tea over which Grandma often presided because April 23 was her birthday. Once, when I was younger, the tea had fallen on a Saturday, so I accompanied her in hopes of glimpsing a dragon. But the closest thing to it was the English-born president of the Ladies Auxiliary, a big bosomed woman in a red rose covered hat who was greatly dismayed to learn I did not hail from jolly old England, but had been born in Vancouver and raised in Grandview! "How utterly provincial," she exclaimed.

"Be proud to be British," said Grandpa that evening. And when I insisted that having been born here, I was Canadian, he ignored me continuing on about the beauty of an English woman's peaches

and cream complexion. As he extolled the fact Britain had the largest empire in the world, I considered asking why he'd left and moved to Grandview, but as he puffed on his ever present pipe he seemed to be elsewhere in thought.